THE WAY OF SOLOMON

FINDING JOY AND CONTENTMENT
IN THE WISDOM OF
ECCLESIASTES

THE WAY OF SOLOMON

RAMI SHAPIRO

HarperSanFrancisco
A Division of HarperCollins*Publishers*

HarperCollins books may be purchased for educational, business, or sales promotional use. For information please write: Special Markets Department, HarperCollins Publishers, Inc., 10 East 53rd Street, New York, NY 10022.

HarperCollins Web Site: http://www.harpercollins.com

HarperCollins®, 📖 ®, and HarperSanFrancisco™ are trademarks of HarperCollins Publishers Inc.

FIRST EDITION

Library of Congress Cataloging-in-Publication Data

Shapiro, Rami M.
    The way of Solomon : finding joy and contentment in the wisdom of Ecclesiastes / Rami Shapiro.—1ˢᵗ ed.
        p.   cm.
    ISBN 0-06-067300-1 (cloth)
    1. Bible.   O.T. Ecclesiastes—Commentaries.   I. Title.
BS1475.3S53   1999
223'.8077—dc21   99-37332
                                                                              CIP

Designed by C. Linda Dingler

04 HADD 10 9 8 7 6 5 4 3

CONTENTS

Acknowledgments

vii

Introduction

1

PART I

THE TEXT

11

PART II

THE TEACHING

93

ACKNOWLEDGMENTS

All life is interdependent; all work is collaborative. I am indebted to my teachers for awakening in me a love of Hebrew and biblical text. I am indebted to my synagogue community for making sure I always have time to write. I am indebted to my family and friends for encouraging me when I am certain I cannot write. And I am indebted to Doug Abrams at HarperSanFrancisco, who believed enough in my writing to share it with you in the form of this book. I am indebted to Doug not only for his willingness to push for the publication of *The Way of Solomon*, but also for his insistence that this be the best book I could offer on the subject. Doug was not contented with what I thought to be a finished book. There were rough edges and loose ends that needed attending to, and he was both kind enough and strong enough to see that I attend to them. This book is the better for his efforts. Doug, thank you.

THE WAY OF SOLOMON

INTRODUCTION

Of all the texts of the Bible, it is Ecclesiastes that speaks to me most powerfully. Traditionally thought to be the mature work of King Solomon, Ecclesiastes offers an honest and hopeful view of life—a refreshing change from the harangues of the prophets and the simple faith of the patriarchs. Solomon speaks with authority, insight, honesty, and compassion. He pulls no punches and does not hide behind simplistic theologies. He is a thousands-year-old sage whose message could not be more timely.

My fascination with Ecclesiastes began in the spring of 1972. I was a student of religion at Smith College in Northampton, Massachusetts—one of eight men studying full-time at the college. I rented one of two rooms on the second floor of a two-story farmhouse at the east end of town. The fellow in the next room was also a religion major, with a concentration in Chinese religion.

While studying Ecclesiastes, this neighbor had stumbled on the fact that the Hebrew word most commonly translated as "vanity" could also mean "emptiness." King Solomon was suddenly transformed in my eyes from Hebrew philosopher to Taoist sage.

I remember the moment he shared this insight with me. He burst into my room and in a voice bubbling with excitement began to translate the text of Ecclesiastes. It was one of the most transformative moments of my life. The idea that Solomon had been crying, "Emptiness! Emptiness upon emptiness!" rather than the well-known "Vanity of vanities!" shook me deeply. Suddenly the whole book of Ecclesiastes changed for me. It shouted at me, clamoring for attention. I could not get the text out of my mind.

I read the book in the original Hebrew and in every English-language version I could find. While no translation dared say what I was hearing from Solomon, the Hebrew continued to throb with new meanings.

For the next ten years I read and studied the text and its commentators. From each commentator I learned something new, and yet each one left me longing for elaboration of that offhand revelation in my Northampton farmhouse. No one saw Solomon as the Hebrew Lao Tzu.

Yet the more I read, the more convinced I became that there was a dimension to Ecclesiastes that was being ignored. I had no desire to reinvent the text or to read into it something that was not there. On the contrary, what I felt called to do was to reveal what was *clearly* there, just overlooked. But it was not enough to simply translate the text. Something more was required.

Ecclesiastes is a testament to the spiritual insights of its author, Solomon. It comes from his deep seeing into the nature of reality. Solomon looked and saw that all is empty of permanence; he also saw that human energies are largely invested in a pursuit of permanence—a pursuit that is doomed from the start. Ecclesiastes is his report of his journey to the heart of reality and his insights into how we should live, given the fact of life's impermanence. The only way to do justice to the text is to follow its author in looking at reality.

In other words, I found that, for me, merely reading the Hebrew and translating it into English was not enough. I had to see for myself if what Solomon had said was true. I had to stand with Solomon and look into the nature of reality alongside him. Then, speaking from the inside out, I could render not simply his words but also his insights into contemporary English.

My work with Ecclesiastes followed three levels of engagement. First, there was a mastery of the text. I could stretch the meanings of the Hebrew, but I could not violate them. Second, there was the study of the commentaries that have grown up around the text. These would reveal the multiple dimensions that other readers of Ecclesiastes have seen and shared for centuries. And third, there was the practice of meditation. It is one thing to understand the ideas Ecclesiastes contains and the mystical commentaries these ideas have engendered. It is another to look for myself and see if what I have read is true.

Solomon was looking beneath the surface of things, and I needed to do the same. What you are reading is, then, not only a translation of the text but also a personal verification of its meaning. I am not simply relating his teaching; I am attesting to its accuracy. I see the wisdom of Solomon as a steadfast guide to living life fully. I apply his teachings to my life daily. They never fail to show me the way to truth, gratitude, contentment, and joy. Solomon's message is not limited to his time; indeed, he speaks as cogently to us as he did to his contemporaries. Our circumstances may differ, but our struggle to understand life and how to live it well is the same.

If Solomon were living today, he would find the world far more complicated than the ancient world he inhabited, yet no more complex. The complexity of life is generated not by the tools we use but by the illusions we cultivate and live by. And the illusions of our day are no different than the illusions of Solomon's time—the illusions of permanence, separateness, and control.

We insist that the world is permanent, and then do all we can to keep ourselves from the truth of its fundamental impermanence.

We insist that each self is not only unique but also separate from every other, and we do all we can to escape from the interdependence of all things.

We insist that life can be controlled, that we can ensure profit for ourselves: financial, moral, spiritual. We then spend our days in the vain effort to control outcomes in our pursuit of wealth, righteousness, and salvation.

Underlying all three illusions is the desire for immortality. Wishing to live forever, we create all kinds of schemes to make that desire seem more and more plausible.

Thus Solomon looked at life and cried, "Emptiness!" All our doings are a vain and ultimately fruitless pursuit of immortality and control. All our theories are futile blustering against the fundamental emptiness of separate things. There is no absolute diversity. There is only the relative diversity of the One manifest as all. Seeing the emptiness of separate things allows us to tap the oneness of all things. And it is this at-one-ment that brings with it the tranquility we so ardently desire.

It is important that we clearly understand this powerful insight from the start. So accustomed are we to reading Ecclesiastes as a negative and harsh critique of human life that we need to make a conscious effort to free ourselves from this misguided view and see the text with fresh eyes.

Saying that reality is fundamentally empty is not the same as saying that life is worthless, meaningless, or without value. On the contrary, when we understand the meaning of emptiness, the essential worth, meaning, and value of every moment are revealed to us.

Several weeks ago a woman came to my office to explore a crisis in her life. She was depressed, lethargic, and without motivation. "My life," she told me, "is empty. I haven't done anything worthwhile with my life." I asked her if she had made breakfast for her children that morning. She had. I asked her if she had fed her cats that morning. She had. I asked her if she had straightened her apartment before coming to see me. She had, and had also thrown in a load of laundry.

"So within the space of a few short hours, you saw to the welfare of two human beings and three felines, and you tidied up a corner of the planet. Not bad for someone whose life is worthless."

She smiled faintly. "That's not what I meant, Rabbi, when I said that my life was worthless. I meant that I haven't done anything *special*. I haven't written a book, or invented anything, or, you know, *done* anything. Nothing big. Nothing important. Nothing lasting. Nothing anyone will remember when I'm gone."

This is the illusion that traps us when we fail to see the fundamental emptiness of things. If we think that permanence is a possibility—if we imagine some kind of immortality for ourselves—we then have to earn it by doing something big with our lives. Something that will cause us to be remembered.

Very few of us will be remembered. And those who are may be remembered wrongly or remembered for horrible things. Immortality through memory is value-free. Hitler and Mother Teresa, for example, both will be remembered. Of course, we could argue that being remembered for doing good is better than being remembered for doing evil, but in the long run immortality through memory does not discriminate. In this view, it is being remembered that counts.

Solomon offers us a different understanding of life. Immortality is an illusion. Memory fades. Doing something great and doing something small are equal in the eyes of eternity. What matters is not our legacy but our capacity to enjoy and honor life here and now. And that capacity is the gift that comes to us with insight into true emptiness.

When we understand that we are not separate from the whole of life, when we understand that there are no separate things, no separate realities, we let go of the urge for personal immortality. We realize that the Whole is birthless and deathless and that we are parts of the Whole.

Imagine an ocean whose surface is dotted with waves. Each wave is unique and distinct. Each has its own shape, space, and time. Each rises and falls in its own way. And yet none is other than the ocean itself. No wave is separate from any other, and all are temporary manifestations of the one ocean.

Now imagine that each wave had a mind of its own, each wave was self-aware and self-conscious. What would the waves be saying to themselves? First, they would compare one wave to another and themselves to all others. This one is taller; that one is fuller. This one is smaller; that one is weaker. Second, they would wonder about the lives of their fellow waves. Third, they would worry about what happens to those waves that seem to die either on the shore or in the midst of their swell. Given enough time, they would create elaborate stories about themselves and what happens to waves after they die. They would embrace those waves they love in a future heaven of shoreless oceans and condemn those they hate to eternal beach.

To us this seems silly. We can see that the wave is just the ocean in extension. We know that when a wave loses its form it simply returns to the ocean, more fully becoming what it always was. It is the illusion of separateness that causes the waves their anxiety. It is their quest for permanence that drives them to worry and judge.

What is true of our hypothetical waves is true also of us. We are the waves of the Divine, of the Infinite, of God. We are God in temporary extension. The extent to which we insist on being other, being permanent and separate from each other and God, is the extent to which we are sad, depressed, anxious, lost, and joyless. The extent to which we see the fundamental emptiness of this illusion and awake to the essential unity of all things in, with, and as God is the extent to which we are alive, vibrant, energized, purposeful, and filled with holy joy.

Ecclesiastes is King Solomon's attempt to reveal the illusion of separateness and awaken us to the wonders of unity. Ecclesiastes seems to be a nihilistic harangue only to those whose allegiance is to the illusion of separateness. To those who can see through Solomon's eyes, those who can see that the wave and ocean are one, Ecclesiastes is a book of liberation holding forth the promise of finding joy in the most ordinary acts of our everyday lives.

When I spoke of this to the woman in my office, she scoffed. She did not want to hear about emptiness and unity with God. She wanted to free herself of the little things in her life so that she might find the time to do the big things she dreamed about, which others might remember. She was in love with her sadness and the illusion that maintained it.

The promise of the book of Ecclesiastes cannot be realized by those in love with sadness and illusion. Ecclesiastes aims to free us from both. And with this in mind, I have set about to render the text into modern English.

I have worked and reworked this version of Ecclesiastes for years. While I am convinced that I can take it no further, I still hold it to be a work in progress. The teachings of this sage cannot be packaged in a single translation (or even a dozen translations). Each reading yields new meanings, insights, and nuances. I would urge any of you who fall in love with Solomon and his teaching to learn Hebrew and read the text in the original. Only then can you hear what I have heard, accompanied by that which only you are privileged to hear.

There is great value in new readings, and I hope that mine does something to bring Ecclesiastes alive in your life. Read my version alongside a standard translation of the text and enter into conversation with the translators. Do not be afraid to question, to argue, to disagree. Do not fear hearing your own message from this master teacher. And do not fear sharing it with others.

The Way of Solomon is divided into two sections. The first section is a complete rendition of Ecclesiastes. By *rendition* I do not mean literal translation in the traditional sense. My concern in presenting this text is more with the meaning implicit in Solomon's words than with the words themselves. There are a host of literal translations available, but all of them fail to tap the heart of Solomon's message.

The second section highlights key passages of Ecclesiastes. These are the portions of Ecclesiastes that speak to me most powerfully. I want you to hear them in isolation, not buried in the rest of the text. Ecclesiastes can be a bit repetitive—repetition being a biblical method of emphasis—but the reader may miss some of Solomon's deepest truths simply because of his presentation. To help avoid that situation, I will focus attention on those teachings that I believe to be the most helpful to modern readers. And to help you grasp what I take to be the message of these passages, I have appended a short essay to each one, offering contemporary examples of the insights in the text.

Read this book slowly. I have divided the pages in such a way as to give each idea its due and to encourage you to attend to the idea carefully. Not every idea will be clear upon first or even second reading. Do not worry. Give the ideas time to take root in your mind. This is not a book of poetry or philosophy, though it contains both. It is a record of the spiritual insights from a sage who looked deep into the nature of reality. It is meant to be savored, carefully considered, and ultimately tested against your own experience.

Whether King Solomon wrote Ecclesiastes himself or it is the work of others who used his name is not important. The power of Ecclesiastes is not in its author but in its message. It is a message seemingly unique in the Bible—a message of hope and contentment based on understanding rather than faith or fear.

The longer I live, the truer the words of Ecclesiastes become. In those words, I find the deepest wellsprings of wisdom. I have done my best to clear a path to this living water. I invite you to drink deeply.

PART I

THE TEXT

These are the teachings of Ecclesiastes,
he who is called the Assembler of Wisdom,
who lived in Jerusalem
during the reign of Solomon,
son of David, king in Jerusalem.

I:I

Emptiness! Emptiness upon emptiness!
The world is fleeting of form,
empty of permanence,
void of surety,
without certainty.
Like a breath breathed once and gone,
all things rise and fall.
Understand emptiness, and tranquility replaces anxiety.
Understand emptiness, and compassion replaces jealousy.
Understand emptiness, and you will cease to excuse suffering
and begin to alleviate it.

I:2

When you are deluded by the illusion of permanence,
you become trapped in the pursuit of profit.
Profit for the body—wealth.
Profit for the mind—knowledge.
Profit for the soul—eternal life.
Vanity and foolishness!
Profit requires permanence, and there is no permanence.
Therefore, there is no profit, and the pursuit of profit yields only
     suffering.

You suffer because you hunger for permanence
and there is only impermanence.
One generation arising from the dust of another,
only to collapse itself in the heap of history.
Even the earth is passing away;
its permanence is an illusion—it passes more slowly than you,
and you mistake its slow death for eternity.
Eternity is not the infinite stretching of time, but the ending of
     time.

When you see the emptiness of things, you see the emptiness of
     time.
When you see the emptiness of time, you are free from eternity.
When you are free from eternity, you no longer pursue
     permanence.
When you no longer pursue permanence, you no longer harvest
     anxiety.
When you no longer harvest anxiety, you reap tranquility.

1:3–4

Cycles, endless rounds, countless turnings—
such is this world under the sun,
your world of imagined separateness and permanence.

The sun climbs eagerly through the sky only to tumble into
    darkness.
It crawls through the night and returns to the climb only to fall
    once more.
The wind blows south, then north;
round upon round of endless spinning.
Rivers pour tirelessly into the sea, and yet the sea is never full.

There is no purpose to it.
Sun, wind, river act according to their nature;
they do what they do because of what they are.
Only you insist upon meaning and purpose.
For you the Way is not enough; for you it must be a Way To
when in fact it is only the Way Of.

Your passion for purpose traps you in the pursuit of
    permanence.
Your hunger for meaning blinds you to the simple beauty of the
    turnings.
There is no tranquility in the Way To;
yet the Way Of is peace itself.

1:5–8

Nothing new arises from the turnings of the world.
What appears new is but a variation of the old.
What appears to be fresh is but the ancient, forgotten and
      rediscovered.
Amnesia feigns creativity, but it has all been before.

You fool yourself, mistaking nuance for newness.
Our generation forgets the rounds of earlier times;
and the next generation will forget the turnings of ours.

There is nothing new—
only forgetfulness masquerading as creativity.

Blessed is the shortness of memory,
for without it we would all go mad.

1:9–11

I, who am called Ecclesiastes, the Assembler of Wisdom,
became a sage among my people.
My reputation for wisdom made me a king in Jerusalem.
My kingdom was the assembled truths of my day.
But I was not satisfied to dwell within her borders,
for what is truth but shared opinion?

So I set for myself the task of exploring Reality,
to see what is even if it disagrees with what we say should be.
I set for myself the task of investigating all matters done in this
        world.
God has suffused this world with suffering,
and I chose to become its chronicler.

1:12–13

I have explored all that is done
in this world of seemingly separate things and selves,
and behold—there is no profit in it.
There is nothing but emptiness, impermanence,
and the vain pursuit of control that arises when you do not see
    the truth.
Control is your addiction,
promising salvation and an end to impermanence.
Rather than enjoy the breeze,
you pursue the wind to bend it to your will.
What madness! What vanity!

1:14

I sought order and found only chaos.
I sought the straight and found only crookedness.
I sought solace and found only suffering.

I said to myself:
My wisdom has grown beyond all who preceded me.
I have delved deep and understood much.
I have chosen the whole of life as my subject:
the wise, the mad, the foolish.
And yet in all my studies I can find no solid ground.
There is no permanence in this world.
And the pursuit of it is but chasing after wind.

Thus do I teach:
The more you seek security, the more you are haunted by
        insecurity.
The more you desire surety, the more you are plagued by
        change.
The more you pretend to permanence, the more you invite
        suffering.
The more you do for control, the less you do for joy.

1:15–18

So I said to myself:
Perhaps it is only wisdom that is folly.
Perhaps in pleasure there is a greater truth and certainty.

But pleasure proved to be no more solid than wisdom;
the body no more stable than the mind.
Laughter is as fleeting as insight,
and joy no more permanent than profit.
Pleasure, no less than knowledge, is fundamentally empty;
and both are without meaning if by meaning we seek
     permanence.

To discover pleasure's emptiness, I first tasted its fullness.
I indulged my flesh and put drink to the test:
Which would quench my deeper thirsts, wine or wisdom?

Not satisfied with the vintage of others,
I planted my own vineyards.
I built grand houses surrounded by gardens and
orchards teeming with fruits of every kind.
I dug pools for irrigation
and seeded forests so thick the ground grew no grass.
I bought men and women to pamper me and maintain my
     mansions.
No one before me had such herds and flocks.

2:1–7

21

I filled my coffers with treasure.
I owned choirs and reveled in their music.
I built stables and raised horses of every breed.
I collected chariots from every nation.
My wealth was without precedent,
and I turned my attention solely to pleasure.
None was more experienced than I in the ways of flesh and
      fortune.

Whatever I desired I took.
I denied myself nothing, and I rejoiced in all I had.
Yes, rejoiced!
Do not pretend there is no joy in ownership or pleasure.
Do not mistake me for one who denies the flesh.
For such is the way of the fool who has nothing and so denies
      desire.
There is desire, and there is pleasure in achieving one's desire.
But there is no permanence.

Pleasure no less than knowledge is empty of permanence
and is thus unable to bring the gift of tranquility.

2:8–10

I looked deeply into all I had acquired:
Where is the certainty?
Where is the permanence?
Where is the meaning that lingers
after the shimmer of profit fades?
And behold, here too I found only emptiness.
The pursuit of pleasure, no less than the pursuit of wisdom,
is but the ego's vain chasing after wind.
There is no permanence in this world under the sun.

Take my word for this,
and waste neither time nor money duplicating my experiment.
You would not be able to draw upon my wealth
and would only end up squandering your own.

I took upon myself the task of exploring the ways of the world,
and I freely share what truth I have found.
Build upon this truth;
do not sift among the ruins.

2:11–13

I compared wisdom with foolishness
to see which is greater.
They are as light and dark—
each the boundary of the other;
each the shadow of the other;
each the complement of the other.
And yet I prefer the light of wisdom to the darkness of folly,
for in it there is discernment,
while darkness makes the jewel seem no more lovely than glass.

The wise can learn from what they see,
whereas the foolish dwell always in ignorance.
Do not imagine, however, that the wise thus earn a greater
      reward,
for the same fate befalls them both.

2:13–14

Do not attach profit to learning
or imagine that permanence comes with wisdom.
There is no permanence in this world,
and that is what the wise ultimately know.
The foolish cling to illusion and race no less slowly to their
    death.

So I said to myself:
If earth swallows both sage and fool,
why should I strive to be wise?

Striving for wisdom in order to find permanence
is its own foolishness.
Striving for permanence through wisdom or folly
is its own madness.
So why be wise?
Because there is no tranquility in foolishness,
while wisdom held lightly can bring peace.
Peace, but not permanence.
Neither the sage nor the fool will be remembered.
In time all is forgotten.
The wise die no less surely than the foolish.

                                        2:14–16

This truth of impermanence haunted me,
and I soured on life.
The suffering of life overwhelmed me,
and I sought refuge in depression.

But I could not escape the truth of what I had seen:
all our doing is in quest of sanctuary from impermanence.
We seek to think our way to certainty;
to buy our way to security;
to pleasure ourselves to eternity.
But nothing brings us the permanence we crave.
Thought is only opinion;
wealth is only a burden;
pleasure is only a prelude to pain.
And in this there is no joy.
We desire not what we have but what does not exist:
permanence, an eternity of self in a world designed by
        selfishness.
It is not wisdom, wealth, or pleasure that brings us pain,
but the mistaking of these for something they are not,
the use of these to grasp something that is not.
Our quest for permanence is the root of our suffering.

2:17

I looked with sorrow on the wealth I had amassed.
Could I possibly spend it all?
Would there be permanence in profit?
Could immortality be purchased or earned?
In the end my wealth will pass to others
and I will die no less penniless than the pauper.

Nor can I take pride in my heirs.
Who is to say if they will be wise or foolish?
Can I control them and their deeds?
Yet they will rule over all I have.
Take no solace in future generations.

Despair swallowed me.
All this labor, all this wealth—and still no peace of mind!
The gold of my coins outlives me.
I labor for heirs I do not know.
How vain to think I could purchase immortality.
How foolish this quest for permanence.
How empty of surety is this world,
and how filled with suffering.

2:18–21

Think on this:
What lasting good do you derive from all your efforts and
	schemes?
What profit outlives the flow of time?
Treasure cannot buy security, nor power lay siege to
	permanence.

If you are trapped in the quest for permanence,
each day boils with anger, frustration, and needless suffering.
Night grants no rest,
and your mind seethes in rage over the theft of security.

You center your world on self;
you pamper yourself with pity;
you delude yourself with vanity—
and none of it gives you what you seek.
For your pursuit of permanence is but the ego's flight from
	truth.
The pursuit is vain,
the prize is mischief,
and in the end all you have is what you are:
emptiness upon emptiness upon emptiness.

2:22–23

If there is no profit to wisdom or folly,
if neither pleasure nor knowledge can bring peace of mind,
what then have I learned?

Simply this:
there is no other good than
eating when hungry,
drinking when thirsty,
and appreciating all that comes your way.
For pleasure and profit are empty as the wind;
there is no lasting joy at all.
Joy is as fleeting as the breeze.
Celebrate its coming, and do not seek to halt its passing away.

2:24

None consumed more lustily than I.
None tasted more pleasure than I.
None grasped more power than I.
Thus it is mine to know
that to the honorable alone are granted grace and simplicity
while to the fool is granted endless hunger for wealth and
control.
The foolish eat and eat and are never filled.
For it is the wind they swallow;
true wealth passes on to others.
Thus do I know that the way of the fool,
the boundless quest for control and permanence
that bolsters the illusion of immortality,
is a fruitless pursuit, a vain chasing after the wind,
leaving you tired, weak, frightened, and alone.

2:25–26

Life is fleeting,
the passing of moments upon moments.
Embrace them as they come;
do not cling to them as they go.
In this alone is there tranquility.
Moments of birth, moments of death;
moments of planting, moments of uprooting;
moments of killing, moments of healing;
moments of knocking down, moments of building up;
moments of mourning, moments of dancing;
moments of casting stones, moments of gathering stones;
moments of embracing, moments of departing;
moments of seeking, moments of forsaking;
moments of keeping, moments of discarding;
moments of tearing, moments of mending;
moments of silence, moments of speech;
moments of love, moments of hate;
moments of war, moments of peace.
Moments and the passing of moments—this is life.
There is a suffering natural to this flow;
there is no escaping either sorrow or joy.
Do not add to the first by clinging to the second,
for in doing so you deny the flow itself.
Live the moment; attend to the doing;
accept whatever comes into your hand.
In this only is the path to tranquility.

3:1–9

The matter of suffering is clear to me:
it arises from ignorance of impermanence.
Everything functions in time;
everything flows, changes, transforms.
In your heart you sense eternity,
but your mind mistakes it for time without end.
Eternity is not endless time;
eternity is the ending of time.
Under the sun it is all flux and flow,
diverse and separate.
But under the sun is not the whole, and
there is a deeper truth
embracing the many in a greater One.

3:10–11

I have understood all this.
And behold, there is nothing more pleasant for you
than to abandon the illusion of permanence
and accept the flow of time,
to accept the moments as they are
and do what you can with each.
When hungry—eat.
When thirsty—drink.
When tired—rest.
When injustice reigns—resist.
When suffering—feel compassion.
In this lies tranquility of body, heart, mind, and soul.

Reality is what It is.
You cannot add to It.
You cannot subtract from It.
When it rains you can shout for the sun,
but the rain will not heed you.
There is only acceptance or rejection.
The first leads to peace; the second, to pain.
God pursues you with peace,
offering each moment for your appreciation.
There is no profit in rejection.
But with acceptance comes tranquility.

3:12–15

From the order of nature
I turned my attention to the order of society.
I looked for justice and found corruption.
I looked for righteousness and found evil.

I said to myself:
Both the righteous and the wicked are haunted by time.
Yet there is a difference.
The righteous accept the flow and find the Way.
Letting go of time, they enter eternity;
letting go of self, they find tranquility.
The wicked insist upon controlling time,
forcing the world to conform to their will.
Theirs is a battle unending. And the prize is only fear.

3:16–17

I thought to myself:
No wonder people say,
The fate of man and beast is the same;
as one dies so dies the other.
There is no advantage.
All are born; all will die.
All arise from dust, and all will return to dust.

And to this thought I added my own:
In our foolish quest to be better than the beast,
we allow ourselves to become even less than the beast.

God tests you with truth—
all things are as empty as the wind.
Will this free you to live,
or frighten you to death?

3:18–20

You pretend that the human soul rises upward
while the beast remains on earth.
What nonsense! What vanity!
The life of one is also in the other.
Both rise and both fall, and everything has its time and its
    season.

Thus I understand the simple truth of life:
there is nothing better than for you to rejoice
in every deed done in harmony with the moment.
For doing is your purpose;
in doing is your meaning.
Leave the result to those who come after you,
and attend solely to doing well that which must be done at all.

3:21–22

I looked further into the world
and observed the oppression caused
by the failure to see the impermanence of self and things.

Pretending to permanence, you seek control,
dominating others to your will.
They cry out for mercy, but your hunger is too great.
You are unmoved by their pain,
and there is no one to comfort them.

So much suffering did I see
that I was ready to praise the dead over the living,
the unborn over the born—
for at least these are beyond the reach of the controlling self.

And all this because you are blind to truth
and bound to the illusion of separate selves and permanence
with which you brand your world.

4:1–3

Look into this carefully.
Why do you labor so hard?
To impress your neighbor?
To blunt the pain of your own mortality?
What vanity!
There is nothing you can own that is not on its way to dust.
The pursuit of permanence is but chasing after wind.

So then, the fool asks, should I abandon work?
This too is nonsense.
Neither labor nor laziness holds the key.

Your problem is not with work but with the fruits of your work.
Better one handful earned with joy than two earned with
        vexation.
Do what you love, and contentment may follow.
Do what you hate, and no amount of wealth will buy you peace.

4:4–6

But labor is not your only folly.
Hoarding what you earn is another madness.

Look—
There are lonely people who sacrifice family and friends
for the riches they think will buy them joy.
Yet they have no time for joy.
For whom do they labor?
Not for themselves, for they have no time for themselves.
Not for others, for they have no time for others;
and if they should have time, there will be no others for them.
Do they labor for the love of labor?
No, for they have no time even to enjoy what they do.
Then why do they labor?
They labor from fear.
They labor to blot out the passing of time and the ending of
        days.
They hope to work themselves out of dying,
when in fact they are already dead to all that matters.
How sad these exhausted fools;
how pathetic those who applaud them.

4:7–8

Here is my advice—learn from one who looked and saw.
Secure yourself a friend; two are better than one.
Do not work alone,
and learn to rejoice in another's company.

If one of you falls, the other is there to help you rise.
If it is cold, you can huddle together for warmth.
If danger threatens, two can face it better than one.
And three better still;
the cord of three strands outlasts the cord of two.

Seek out companions for work.
Seek out friends for life.
Make room for yourself and also for others.

4:9–12

Be careful from whom you seek advice.
Do not be fooled by appearance.
Set no authority over yourself save Reality,
for in Reality alone does truth reside.

There is a young beggar wise beyond her years.
From her you should ask.
There is a great king who no longer exercises caution.
From him you should not ask.

It is not age but wisdom that matters.
It is not power but restraint that makes the sage.

4:13

Be careful whom you place in power.
There is a man newly out of prison, yet wise and kind.
Let him rule.
Or a pauper without influence, yet rich in wisdom and
    compassion.
Let her rule.

I saw this happen:
A youth was raised to be king by one generation
and rejected by the next.
His wisdom carried him to power,
but his modesty failed to fill the people's hunger for power and
    display.
They brought him down not because he could not guide them,
but because he would not dominate them.

Leaders, gurus, sages—this too is but chasing after wind.

4:14–16

42

Be careful when drawing near to God.
Seek not to sacrifice or appease;
seek only to hear.

The fool rushes in to sacrifice,
hoping to buy what is free to all.

Better to stand silent and listen.
Better to be taught by Silence than distracted by teaching.
Better to receive wisdom than to give in to illusion.

4:17

When standing before God,
you rush to speak, your heart bursting with needs and urgency.
You crowd the air with words of praise and pleading.
You leave no room for Silence and none for hearing.
It is not God you worship, but your own voice and opinion.

Better to stand in Silence.
Do not rush your words, but seek to quiet them.
With a quiet mind, a heart still and silent,
you will see the infinity of God and the finity of self.
Humility will embrace you,
and you will fade into That Which Is All That Is.
Your words will be few;
the Silence, great.
There is room then for listening.

5:1

Just as dreams flood the sleeping mind,
so words engulf the waking mind.

When you promise something to God, do that thing quickly.
Delay makes fools of good intentions.
You are only as good as your pledge.

Better to promise nothing
than to fulfill no promise.

Do not allow your mouth and body to betray each other,
promising one thing while doing another.
Your reputation will suffer,
and all your deeds come under suspicion.

5:2–5

What to do with the noise of your dreams?
What to make of the chattering of your mind?
Cultivate the Silence that comes
from knowing the emptiness
and impermanence of all things.

5:6

Be not surprised by the corruption of government—
oppressing the poor,
perverting justice,
scoffing at righteousness.
This is to be expected when one rules another
and is in turn ruled by the desire to rule.

Power over another leads to corruption of self.
Seek no power;
claim no authority.

What you own ultimately owns you.
That to which you cling strangles you.

You think that ownership is freedom,
but I say this: Even a king becomes enslaved to the soil.

5:7–8

You think that wealth will make you free.
But I say this: Freedom is not bought, but seized.
Freedom is not the last step, but the first.
You never have enough money.
You never have enough possessions.
You become enslaved to owning
and suffocate beneath a mountain of debt and fancy debris.

The more you have, the more you are hounded.
The more you have, the more you have to defend;
and you will have no time for appreciation and joy.

Sweet is the sleep of those honest workers
who find satisfaction in their lot.
But the desire of those enslaved to more
rumbles loud and prevents tranquility.

5:9–11

I have witnessed a great suffering in this world.
You pretend to labor for others,
but your work becomes an escape from others.
Your wealth becomes your enemy.
If the wealth is lost to error or stolen by thieves,
there is nothing left of you.
You can give your children nothing:
neither gold nor love is yours to give.

You come into the world naked.
You leave it naked as well.
Empty we enter; empty we depart.
You waste your time trying to find fullness in things or desires.
What fullness there is arises of its own accord
when you learn to live simply with whatever each moment
        brings.

Here is the root of your suffering: chasing permanence.
It is a race for the wind, and you drop exhausted from the chase.
You thought to make something of yourself
and to leave something behind.
But there is nothing to make and nothing to leave.

5:12–15

What is the profit of all your efforts?
You eat in darkness,
your eyes clouded with worry.
Your days are scarred by anxiety, illness, and anger.
Nothing is as we insist it be.
Everything is as it is meant to be.
Insist on its being different
and you commit yourself to needless suffering and resentment.
Accept what is and discover what might yet come to be.

5:16

What shall you do?
Work yourself to distraction?
Distract yourself from work?
Neither extreme is desirable.
Better the middle way:
eat and enjoy your food in the company of friends;
work and enjoy the capacities of body and mind.
In this world of seeming separation and divided minds,
there is no escape from impermanence.
Do not build a fortress against loss
or lay siege to eternity.
Rather, open your eyes to the wonder of the fleeting
and make of each moment an opportunity to do what needs
        doing.

Your days are few and
you cannot know which will be your last.
Appreciate the moment.
Sharpen your mind.
Live with attention.
Live without expectation.
And let sorrow and joy take care of themselves.

5:17–19

Suffering is a part of life,
but you add to it and make it so much worse.

I say this:
You labor hard and become wealthy.
You own much and are admired by many.
But the cost is high—
you have no time to enjoy your success.
Your days are spent adding and defending,
and the fear of loss crowds out the joy of gain.

To acquire in hopes of finding peace is foolish.
Even if you live a hundred years, even if death never touches
        you,
if you seek peace through possessions you will find only
        bitterness.
Better to be born dead
than to kill yourself in pursuit of peace through possessions.

                                                    6:1–3

The stillborn arrives empty and departs empty.
The pain of her passing is her parents', not her own.

The fool who births a fortune in hopes of buying peace is worse
        off,
for the pain of emptiness is his.

Even if you live one thousand years,
if you seek to escape suffering through wealth
you only add to the pain and rob yourself of joy.

And in the end the stillborn and the wealthy meet in death—
the one still empty and at peace;
the other still grasping, gasping, and wild.

                                                    6:4–6

At first you work to fill your belly,
but the hunger never wanes.
No wisdom ends it;
no folly fills you up.

One who places hope in work, saying,
—"My effort shall be counted and bring me reward,"
is no better than one who roots hope in suffering, saying,
——"My pain shall be noted and bring me compensation."
Both seek to control tomorrow, and in this they are equally
    foolish.

Your fate is set at birth:
all who are born are fated to die.
Neither wealth nor poverty can change that.
It is death that haunts you—death, impermanence,
    meaninglessness.
You cannot buy your way out of these.
You cannot barter poverty for peace.
Neither possessions nor the avoidance of possessions brings joy.
Only touch both lightly,
clinging to nothing and
entering fully into the passing moment and what it brings.

6:7–10

54

There are so many things to which you can cling.
All of them bring suffering, for clinging is the cause of suffering.

Do not listen to friends who tell you: Buy this and you will feel
    better.
Their advice only leads you deeper into shadow.
The light of truth cannot be purchased.
It is free to all who would but step into it.

Do not be misled by those who promise reward in the world to
    come.
This is ego and vanity, a chasing after wind.
Be not distracted from the moment.
Do right in this world and let the rest take care of itself.

6:11–12

Better to be honored for what you do
than valued for what you own.

Better the day of death than the day of birth;
for death ends the illusion of permanence
while birth ignites it.

Better to go to a house of mourning
than to a house of feasting.
In the first there is the silence of death,
the transience of life, the tears of loss and letting go.
This is the world, its simplicity and its suffering.
In the other there is only blind hunger,
forced laughter, false joy—
a desperate filling up of that which is forever emptying.
In the first there is truth, which leads to love.
In the second there is illusion, which leads to lust.

7:1—2

Better a serious posture than a lighthearted pose.
The first leads to self-reflection and truth;
the second, to foolishness and self-deception.

The wise are drawn to the house of mourning,
welcoming the cleansing of illusion and desire
that grief entails.

The foolish rush to the house of laughter,
hoping to find joy in making fun.

Better the reproof of the wise
than the praise of fools.
The first empties you of self.
The second fills you with pride.

7:3⁻5

The joy of fools is like the crackling of thorns
under a cooking fire.
They make much noise and provide little heat.

Do not be fooled by the foolish.
Their joy is forced;
their laughter, a bandage for despair.
It is easy to become snared in their illusion,
but doing so warps your understanding and brings only pain.

Contemplate endings over beginnings, and
remember that impermanence is the Way of all things.

Better patience than overconfidence—
allowing what is to ripen into what will be
rather than seeking conformity to your own desires.

Rush not to anger,
for anger closes the eye to truth
and blinds you to the evil you do.

7:6–9

Do not compare one day to another.
Make what you can of each day as it is.

It is good to have both wealth and wisdom,
though do not imagine that either will bring you peace.

Knowledge guards the mind from deception.
Wealth protects the body from hunger.
But only acceptance of impermanence brings tranquility.

7:10–12

Consider the workings of Reality;
learn to set right what you have done wrong.

There is good. There is evil.
And both dwell within you.

When you do right, rejoice,
but do not proclaim yourself righteous.
This was but one moment;
in the next you may do differently.

When you do wrong, reflect,
but do not call yourself evil.
This was but one moment;
in the next you can do differently.

For this is the Way of Reality: good and evil entwined as one.
Deny neither;
take responsibility for both;
and live with integrity.
When you die you will leave only dust behind.

7:13–14

I have seen everything from the eyes of impermanence.
There is no salvation in righteousness
or escape from suffering in evil.
There is no reward. There is no punishment.
There is only the coming and going of life.

I have seen good people needlessly die despite their goodness.
I have witnessed the wicked triumph despite their wickedness.
And there is no explanation.

Seek no salvation in wisdom and no solace in folly;
only accept what is moment to moment.
Salvation demands permanence, and both wisdom and folly are
        delusions of the mind.
Those who seek salvation in wisdom and righteousness
never become truly wise or truly righteous.
Their desire to escape impermanence
destroys their capacity for joy.
In the end they die,
anxious, exhausted, fearful, and
no less troubled for all their learning.

                                        7:15–16

Do not consciously pursue evil,
for in this too there is no salvation.
You will err enough without trying;
why court an early death when death comes soon enough?

Better to accept both goodness and evil
and know your capacity for both.
In this way you avoid pride and prejudice,
being thankful for the good you achieve and
making amends for the evil you do.

Do not rend the spiritual and the material.
There is but one road in Life, and all walk upon it.
Both body and soul walk this path,
and you walk it best when they walk it together.

One who understands Reality
speaks neither of body nor of soul;
but only of That which manifests them both.

7:17–18

Be wary of wisdom not rooted in Reality.
There is no one easier to fool than yourself.

Though wisdom be more powerful than armies,
nothing can protect you from making mistakes.

The righteous too do evil,
and even the wicked have accomplished some good.
Good and evil are a part of all things.
Wisdom that does not reveal your responsibility for both is not
      wise.

                  7:19–20

Be not oversensitive to what you hear.
Even those who love you curse you now and again.
Listen not, nor dwell on momentary angers.

For you know in your heart
that your thoughts are tainted
and your lips too speak evil.

7:21—22

I have exhausted the wisdom of the sages.
I have observed every aspect of life under the sun.

I had hoped to go beyond these,
but I found a limit to the mind.

I had thought to probe the deeper truths:
What was the world before it was the world?
What is the purpose of all that was, is, and will come to be?

But these are truths beyond thought and observation,
and before them we must be silent.

7:23–24

So I returned to what can be known
and looked again at the doings of humankind.
I sought to uncover more clearly that which drives us.
I sought to see more clearly
the nature of wickedness, foolishness, folly, and madness.
For I sensed that a common cause underlies them all:
a passion for permanence that pits us against Truth.

And in this I came first to sex.
More bitter than death
are the treacheries we inflict in pursuit of sex.

It is a snare, a trap, a noose—
in sex we glimpse true emptiness,
the passing and impermanence of all things.
For an instant the self dies
and there is a greater knowing.
But the instant bursts and we doubt our own knowing,
racing after confirmation as if sex could save.

Passion for unity that is the momentary gift of sexual union
distracts us from the deeper emptiness that is the gift of lasting
    union.

7:25–27

Why is this wisdom so rare among us?

God fashions us with the capacity
to know truth and do good;
but we devise many schemes
to promote ignorance and excuse evil.

7:28–29

None compares to one who knows the Way of all things.
Such knowing brings light to the face
and softens all one's features.

So let me counsel you:
Adhere to the Way and attend to Reality.

Do not run from truth,
insisting upon bending what is to conform to what you desire.
Reality is what *is*; it is you who must do the bending.

For Reality flows of its own accord.
Power belongs only to That Which Is;
you cannot bend the whole.

8:1–4

One who attends solely to Reality
avoids unnecessary suffering
and intuits the Order that binds the chaos of the world.

For there is order to everything,
despite the evil one perceives.

Those who persist in illusion,
seeking permanence and control,
have their moment of reckoning.
They know this and cannot shake the knowing.
They fear it and cannot escape the fear.
What they do not know is that the fear itself is the reckoning.

Just as you cannot command the wind,
just as you cannot ward off death,
just as you cannot ensure peace,
so you cannot escape the consequences of your deeds:
evil consumes evil; good invites good.

8:5–8

All this have I seen as I studied the role of power in the world.
Whenever you seek power over another,
no matter how politely you excuse it, it is seeded with evil.

There is no power over destiny;
neither the wicked nor the wise control it.

I have seen the name of the vile revered by their children,
and the memory of the just forgotten
even by those blessed by their deeds.
There is no sense and no reward—
to think otherwise is delusion.

Some see the success of the wicked
and follow their lead,
seeking riches through evil.
Sometimes it works.
But in the end, evil eats itself and those who serve it.

The wicked cannot abide by truth,
so they construct a world of lies
that ultimately collapses of its own weight,
crushing them beneath the folly of their own illusions.

8:9–13

There is no sense to this world:
the righteous suffer while the wicked thrive.
To expect things to conform to your logic is foolish;
Reality is not of your making.

Therefore, cease your agonizing and rejoice.
There is nothing better for you than this:
eat and enjoy what you eat;
drink and enjoy what you drink.
Do this and tranquility will accompany you
throughout your trials and
through all the days of your life under the sun.

8:14–15

When I set myself to observe and study
all that passes for wisdom,
to perceive all that takes place on earth,
and to uncover the Way of Reality
that is written on the heart of every being,
I realized that I cannot reduce the Whole
to the limits of the part.

The ordinary person cannot fathom the Way.
Nor can the wise uncover it.
And any who pretend to know
are themselves fools or worse.

8:16–17

I meditated deeply on all I observed,
and it became clear to me that
no one controls his or her destiny—
not the wise,
not the simple.
Though we cannot be certain of what the next moment will
        bring—
love or hate, violence or calm—
we can be sure that in time
it will bring all to our doorstep.

9:1

All things come to all people.
The righteous no less than the wicked
feel the sting of suffering.
The evil no less than the good
taste the dew of love.
The impious no less than the religious
find the grace of God.
The kind no less than the heartless
boil with rage.
The honest no less than the liars
fall to the con man's snare.

It seems wrong that the same fate comes to all.
You want rewards and punishments in accordance with what
        you do.
You want a prize cherished by all but reserved for the few.
But who are you to want or denounce?
You who live under the sun in a world deluded by divisions,
        dogma, ego.
Madness comes from your self-obsession.
Only death ends the struggle for permanence.
Mercy comes from not dividing
from moving beyond the limitations of self.

9:2–3

Even the most pious cannot be certain of eternity.

Better a living dog than a dead lion.
Do not live this life as a prelude to the next.

The only surety for the living is dying.
The dead know nothing;
the self fades;
memory no longer freezes moments into eternities;
all reward is abandoned, and only silence reigns.

Your loves, your hates, your jealousies—all gone,
for these are the stirrings of a restless mind
deluding itself with autonomy and isolation.

The dead relinquish this delusion
and let go their grasping after illusion.

Better to die now while you still live
than to live now enslaved to fear of death.

9:4–6

Dying now—go eat your bread in simplicity, appreciation, and
    joy.
Drink your wine with a heart unburdened by yesterday and
    tomorrow.
Reality takes care of itself.
You are simply its means; leave the ends to God.

Do not seek to escape the ordinary.
Do not denigrate the body.
Keep your clothing clean and your appearance neat.
Do not pretend to holiness, for all are befuddled by Reality.

Live joyfully with a lifelong companion.
Accept the impermanence of all things.
Accept the interdependence of all things.
Seek not to escape your fate,
but embrace whatever you encounter with
simplicity, humility, grace, courage, honesty, and humor.
Labor and love as best you can,
welcoming success as well as suffering.

Heed my words well:
There is nothing better than this.

9:7–9

Whatever is given you to do,
do it with full attention.
Withhold neither body nor mind,
but allow Life to consume you.
Like a log aflame and tended,
give warmth, light, comfort, and fuel,
and in the end leave only ash.

For there is neither deed nor planning,
neither knowledge nor wisdom,
in the grave where you are going.

Seek not to buy your way out of the grave.
Seek only to spend yourself wisely in life.

9:10

Again it is clear to me
that in this world of separate selves and willful minds
there is no rhyme or reason.

The race goes not to the swift;
the battle goes not to the brave;
bread is won not by wisdom;
wealth is earned not by creativity;
fame comes not to the learned;
and everything is chaos, flux, change, and madness.

You do not know the length of your life,
and you hide from death behind the illusion of immortality.

Just as a fish is taken in a net,
just as a bird is caught in a snare,
so are you trapped in the illusion of permanence.

9:11–12

Do not look to wisdom to avoid the trap.

I have heard of a small city besieged by a powerful king.
The city survived by the genius of a poor man,
and now no one even remembers his name.

So wisdom is greater than armies,
yet fame is bestowed upon those with the trappings of power.

The words of the wise are spoken in quiet,
yet their silence is more effective than the shouts of kings.

Wisdom is better than weapons;
but, misused, it is no less evil.

9:13

It takes but one dead fly to spoil a jar of the finest perfume;
it takes but one foolish act to sour a life of wisdom and honor.

The wise learn to channel passion to serve their purpose.
The foolish mistake passion for purpose and are forever at its
    mercy.

Even if the foolish choose a path to follow,
it is quickly abandoned as another suddenly appears more
    alluring.

This is the sign of the fool:
no purpose,
just passion.

10:1–3

Seek not to dominate others.
You cannot control even yourself.
The pursuit of control is a quest tainted with terror.

Do not excuse evil with reference to intent.
The thought does not count,
and your actions have consequences.
You have choice now and now again;
the responsibility for what you do is yours alone.

The quest for control elevates the foolish to power;
they sit upon the high places and pretend to rule the sea.
The wise sit in the low places and allow the waters to gather
        naturally.

A fool in power appoints a greater fool to advise.
And with this, the just order is overturned.

10:4–7

Those who set traps for others
will themselves be trapped.

Those who shatter the moral order
will themselves be bitten by the snake of injustice.

Those who set stones to trip another
will themselves slip and fall.

Those who loose an avalanche of logs to crush another
will themselves be crushed.

If the axe is blunt, it requires enormous effort to wield it.
Wiser to sharpen the blade and
do what needs doing with the least effort.

If a charmed snake is allowed to strike,
of what value is the charmer?
If learned people act on whim,
of what value was their teacher?

10:8–10

The words of the wise are a beacon to others,
opening the eyes of the blind.
The words of the fool darken the sight
even of those who have never seen light.

From the first word the fool is lost,
mistaking the word for the thing,
the dream for the truth;
and in the end there is only madness.

The foolish multiply words,
hiding their lies in a tower of confusion.

The future cannot be revealed, only encountered.
The past cannot be changed, only accepted.
The present requires action and attention,
but to this the fool is oblivious.

The foolish are exhausted by their own scheming
and cannot find their way to truth.

10:12–15

Pity the nation ruled by the inexperienced.
The foolish rush the palace and feast on its treasures,
while the people starve for lack of vision.

Happy is the nation guided by wisdom,
her leaders living by truth,
using her wealth for goodness,
and not becoming drunk on power.

Where the leader is lazy, the ceiling collapses.
Where the workers are uncaring, the walls leak.

The foolish mistake power for purpose,
wine for joy,
money for salvation.
Yet so great is their fear
that they watch every tongue.

In a land of fools, beware of criticizing the rich and powerful—
not even in your mind, not even to your spouse—
for your words will fly like birds,
and your thoughts will doom you.

10:16–20

Toss your bread upon the sea—
your fate to unfold as it will.

Cast a net of kindness far and wide.
Worry not about profit;
simply do what is right with compassion.

The future is uncertain;
you can plan, but there is no promise.
Do not invest your money in a single venture.
Divide your wealth among seven, even eight investments.
You cannot know which will prosper and which will fail.

There is an order to nature.
Storm clouds spill their rain.
A fallen tree does not stand up.
A dead dog does not bark.
But there is no such certainty in human affairs.
Act without hesitation;
do what is right without thought of reward or consequence.

11:1–4

There is no surety in this world.
You cannot know the way of the wind:
the weather does not follow your desires or predictions.

You cannot know the fate of an embryo in its mother's womb.
Pray all you want; the child's fate is not yours to control.

Just as your eye cannot see itself,
so you cannot know the workings of God.
Therefore, commit yourself to justice and mercy from your
      youth;
do not become lax in old age.
You are the doing of the world—do what is right.

You cannot predict success or avoid failure.
Act without reward, and the act will be your reward.

11:5–6

Rejoice in the awesome beauty of nature:
it is a balm for the eyes to watch the sun rise.

Life itself is wonder.
As long as you live,
live in awe.
And remember—
some days are bright, others are dark,
and both are life's shadow play.
Make no snare for the light;
there is no salvation in holding on.
Make no drama of the dark;
there is no reward for suffering.
Rather, embrace each as it is,
knowing that true joy
resides in serving each moment in peace.

11:7–8

To the youth I say: Rejoice!
Revel in your youth,
let your heart run wild,
and embrace life fully;
drink life deeply.
Follow the passions of your heart.
Heed the desire of your eyes.
But do not expect wisdom from this,
or be sure of success.

As you age,
do not lament the passing of passion
or the weakening of sight.
There is a bliss that comes with aging,
but it is lost to those who insist on youth beyond its time.

Remove anger from your heart,
and banish evil from your actions.

Childhood and youth are fleeting.
Enjoy them when they come,
but do not hold them tight when they are ready to go.

11:9–10

How shall you live,
in youth and in age?
Keep God with you always;
let the One Who Is All shine through all who are one.

Walk with God in youth,
bend with God in age;
and your last days will be
no less than your first.

When the end-times come
and you have no desire for tomorrow,
be neither angry nor despairing;
know that all things come to pass
arising from and returning to
the One Who Is the Source and Substance of All.

12:1

Before the light is harsh to your eye;
before your eye dims to the glory of sun, moon, and stars;
before the clear sky seems clouded;
before your limbs tremble and your back is bent;
before your teeth blunt and your eyes fog;
before your bowels tighten and your stomach slows;
before your sleep is fitful and your ears seem stuffed with cloth;
before the slightest incline seems like a great mountain;
before the easiest task becomes a great challenge;
before tumors threaten and boils erupt;
before your spine twists and you cannot stand erect;
before sexual desire fails;
before your mind dwells on death and your friends appear as
        mourners;
before your bones become brittle and your thoughts muddled;
before your connection to this world is severed
and the dust of you returns to the earth
and the breath of you returns to the One Who Breathes Us All;
Before all this, know:

The whole of life is empty of permanence;
there is no certainty,
no surety,
no salvation to lift you out of impermanence.
There is only doing without reward;
serving without payment;
learning without knowing;
rejoicing without reason;
loving without controlling;
walking without map and measure.
To think otherwise is to pursue the wind,
and vanity piles upon vanity
as you seek to freeze that which is forever melting.

12:2–8

90

EPILOGUE

Solomon was both sage and teacher.
He weighed our thoughts
and probed our actions.
His insights seeded many proverbs.

He revealed valuable knowledge,
sharing the keys to correct living and true understanding.

The words of the wise guide us to right living.
They are like well-fastened nails with broad heads
holding boards fast to their place.
And they all come from the One Who Guides Us All.

Do not seek surety in wisdom.
Exercise caution in the pursuit of knowledge,
for it too can trap you in the vanity of imagined permanence.
There is no end to the buying of books,
and thus no end to their being written.
Study can become a burden of its own,
robbing you of strength and joy.
For in the end there is no certainty that the mind can grasp,
and security is not for us born under the sun.

In sum, the Assembler taught us well:
stand in wonder before God,
and deal justly and kindly with all that come our way.

Cling to nothing and allow all to pass;
and do not imagine that you can buy your way to eternity.
You cannot control destiny,
nor can you secure reward;

yet God brings every deed to fruition,
allowing even the hidden motive its due.
Whether for good or for ill,
the consequences of your deeds will manifest;
you will reap what you sow;
and Order will use Chaos as it will.

So when all is said, remember this:
open your mind to wonder,
your heart to compassion,
and your hand to justice,
that you fashion a whole and holy world.

12:9–14

PART II

THE TEACHING

EMPTINESS UPON EMPTINESS!

Emptiness! Emptiness upon emptiness!
The world is fleeting of form,
empty of permanence,
void of surety,
without certainty.
Like a breath breathed once and gone,
all things rise and fall.
Understand emptiness, and tranquility replaces anxiety.
Understand emptiness, and compassion replaces jealousy.
Understand emptiness, and you will cease to excuse suffering
and begin to alleviate it.

1:2

The key to understanding Ecclesiastes—indeed, the key to understanding life—lies in this first sentence: *havel havalim,* emptiness upon emptiness. Unless we understand this theme, which is central to Solomon's insights into life and how to live it well, we cannot fully benefit from his teaching.

The word *emptiness* is often misunderstood as denoting a state of being that is worthless, meaningless, valueless, useless, and unreal. Reflecting that misunderstanding, many translations of this passage refer to *vanity* or *futility*. Reading Ecclesiastes with that interpretation would lead us to the conclusion that Solomon's view of life is depressive, nihilistic, and not worth studying. After all, most of us are looking for a perspective that is uplifting—one that values life and teaches us how to live it with dignity, joy, and inner peace. If Solomon is telling us from the start that life is worthless, there is no need for us to proceed further.

Unfortunately, this reading of Ecclesiastes is far too common. I say *unfortunately* for two reasons. First, it does the book an injustice. By misreading *havel havalim* as *vanity* or *futility*, we rob the text of its true message. Second, it does the reader an injustice. By assuming Solomon to be despairing of life and condemning of all our efforts to make something of it, we deprive ourselves of Ecclesiastes' liberating insight into the true nature of life and its powerful message of how to live with joy and tranquility.

Far from being the nihilistic rantings of a depressed sage, Ecclesiastes is a brilliant paring away of our illusions about life in order to free our energies and focus our attention on those things that will bring tranquility and hope into our lives. Solomon is not despairing of life. On the contrary, he celebrates life, and he knows exactly how to live it well. What concerns him is our failure to understand life correctly.

Without right understanding of the nature of reality, we are confused, and in our confusion we tend to expend our energies on things that seem to promise joy but deliver only frustration. Our efforts are wrongly focused and cannot help but fail to get us what we want. This consequence may leave us depressed and despairing, something Solomon wants to help us avoid.

Ecclesiastes, then, is a guide that suggests how to embrace reality with joy and contentment. Solomon's goal is twofold. First, to help us clearly see the nature of life. Second, to offer us a strategy for engaging life—a strategy that will, if we have the courage to follow it, bring us a deep sense of peace.

So what is this right understanding of life? Life is *havel havalim*—not vain and futile, as most translators put it, but empty of separate and permanent selves and open to constant change and surprise. In Hebrew, the phrase *havel havalim* literally means "breath of breaths." In other words, life is no more substantial than a breath. It is fleeting, ephemeral, impermanent. The world is in a state of constant flux: everything changes; nothing stays the same.

This is true of ourselves as well as of the world around us. We too are in a constant state of flux. There is nothing about us that is permanent; we have no permanent self to protect or perfect. At first we may find this idea frightening. Because we long for a self that is unchanging—a *me* that is unique, separate, and permanent—the idea that such a self is an illusion leaves us anxious and agitated.

If we have the courage to really listen to what Solomon is saying, however, we will find that the absence of permanence is the most liberating insight of all. Far from denying the value of self, Ecclesiastes frees the self from fixed forms and allows us to recreate ourselves over and over again in order to embrace life fully and joyously.

When leading workshops in Ecclesiastes, I often ask participants to bring with them photographs of themselves at various stages of life. People bring in baby pictures, pictures of themselves on their first bicycle, high school and college graduation photos, wedding photos. I ask them to review the photos in chronological order and take a look at the flow of their lives. I give them a few minutes to relive a memory and connect with the person in each photograph. Then I ask them, "Is the person in the earliest photograph the same person who is in the latest photograph?"

"Of *course* it's the same person," they answer. "It's *me*." This seems true enough on the surface, but in fact it is quite misleading. The *me* we identify with in the earliest photographs is hardly the *me* we see in the latest photographs. Whether we are speaking biologically, emotionally, or intellectually, the *me* in each photograph is quite different from the *me* in all the others. Yes, the DNA signature and fingerprints of each photo subject are constants; but if that is all we mean when we say *me*, there is far less meaning in being *me* than even the most depressed reading of Ecclesiastes would suggest!

When we say *me*, we are referring to something substantial, something conscious, something intrinsically stable, something we can count on and take pride in, something that we hope (secretly or openly) is immortal. It is this self and this hope that Ecclesiastes wishes to challenge.

I usually share my own set of photographs during this part of the workshop. I have a picture of me as a baby wearing a sailor suit, a photo of me with my mom helping me navigate the sidewalk in front of our house, another of me riding a bicycle, one from my high school yearbook, several from college, grad school, and rabbinical seminary, and one taken a few years ago with my dad in Jerusalem. I hold up the sailor suit *me* and the Jerusalem *me*. Some forty-plus years separate these two photographs. Is the *me* in the first photo the same *me* we see in the last photo? I don't think so.

Every seven years or so almost every cell in our bodies has been replaced, so physically the *me* in the sailor suit is several bodies removed from the *me* in Israel. In addition, each of us experiences an emotional deepening and a maturing over time; the feelings of a baby boy are not those of a forty-five-year-old man. So in that sense, too, we have photos of two very different people. And intellectually there is more disconnection than connection between the two people in these photos. By every meaningful measure, then, we are looking at two different individuals. What is true of my photos is true of everyone else's as well. Yet each of us continues to say of our earliest photos as well as the later photos, "This is me."

What is the *me* that carries over from picture to picture, from year to year?

Many people will argue that the real *me* is the soul. They posit a nonphysical self that inhabits the various selves depicted in the photographs. I am not going to argue for or against this idea. All I will suggest is that if this soul is not physically recognizable as *me*, if it is not my emotional self or my intellectual self, then whatever it may be is so far removed from the *me* that I think I am when I refer to myself as *me* as to be incapable of providing me with the sense of continuity and permanence that I am seeking in life.

This can be a difficult idea to grasp. We most often use the word *soul* in a manner that implies a permanent self. Depending upon one's particular belief system, it is the soul that lives on after the body dies. It is the soul that is judged after death. It is the soul that endures punishment in hell or reward in heaven. It is the soul that transmigrates from body to body in the slow evolutionary quest for enlightenment. But if the soul is not the *me* that I take myself to be, then in what way does it matter to me what happens to the soul after this *me* is gone?

The subject of reincarnation often comes up at my lectures. While most of the people I meet have abandoned belief in a literal heaven or hell, many of them are more than willing to place their trust in reincarnation. When they speak of reincarnation, however, they are not thinking in terms of the Hindu understanding of reincarnation, which allows us to be reborn in hellish worlds no less horrible than anything imagined by Dante or Bosch; rather, they are anticipating a never-ending return to human form from which they can continue their quest for life's ultimate meaning.

Again, without arguing the truth or falsehood of reincarnation, I question whether this idea of transmigrating souls does what we need it to do if it is to provide us with the security of having a separate and permanent self. The subtle message of reincarnation is that the self we think we are, the self we love and cherish and wish to live forever, is not our *true* self. Something other than the *me* I see when I look into a mirror moves from life to life. The problem is that if this soul is not the *me* I think of when I refer to the *me* I am, it cannot satisfy my need for permanence. I do not want a *true me* to live forever; *I* want to live forever.

Many people who place their faith in reincarnation or other soul theories of life after death fail to examine just what it is that survives death. They want to believe that they personally will survive death, that the ego is immortal, that there is a continuity of consciousness from one life to the next or from one world to the next that will allow them to look into a mirror and say to the only *me* they know, "You will not die."

Yet the self we identify with here and now is defined by the content of its consciousness, and this content is limited to this life and the memories we retain of it. If I was, say, an African woman killed by a lion in a previous life, while in this life I am a male descendent of white Eastern European Jews, in what sense is the *I* that I wish to transcend death the *I* that I see when I look in the mirror? Whatever this supposedly transcendent self may be, it is not the *me* I really wish to be immortal. I do not want some other *me* to live on; I want the *me* that I know myself to be to live on.

I have friends who believe that whole families reincarnate together. Their son was once their mother, and their mother was once their father, and so on. If this is so, then who are they *really*?

If I believed in separate selves and reincarnated souls, the comfort I would seek from such a belief would be negated by the very dynamics of reincarnation itself. If the woman I love in this life used to be my great-grandfather in a past life and might be reborn as someone else in my next life, in what sense am I comforted by knowing that we will be together in the next life? I do not want to be reunited with my great-grandfather; I want to be reunited with *her*, the woman I love in this life. If over time she has been my lover, friend, sibling, parent, and grandparent, whatever *she* is is not what I long for at all.

In other words, all this talk about self, soul, reincarnation, and life after death is, to my mind, an escape from the simple fact of impermanence that Solomon is asking us to explore, and does not really satisfy the ego's craving after permanence and personal immortality at all.

The person I am at this very instant has no past and no future. I exist only in this moment. And this moment is over before I can even acknowledge it. The transience of moments undercuts the consistency of self. But without a sense of consistency, I fear I would go mad. So I tell a story that links one *me* to the next to maintain the comforting illusion of constant selfhood.

It is the story that sustains us. It is also the story that blinds us to the truth: outside the world of narrative, there is no self other than who we are at this moment, and this moment, and this moment. All there is is freshness, newness, birth/death/rebirth in a burst of time that lasts no longer than a breath of air.

If we understand this—not just intellectually but on a deeper, more transformative level—we can embrace the present with a freshness of body and mind that allows us to find each moment of life, even those that are painful and sad, an opportunity for blessing and joy.

Is Solomon telling us that we must live without a story? No. But when we understand the nature of storytelling as a means of inventing the self, we no longer find ourselves trapped in the tale. We can appreciate the story for what it is (a necessary fiction) and not imagine it to be more than it is (the absolute truth).

It is this freedom from the story that offers us so much hope. Free from the story, we are free to discover ourselves anew in each moment. There is no past to replicate or future to anticipate. There is only this present moment and our embracing of it. And in this very moment there is the potential for clarity of insight and quiet joy that can be found nowhere else.

Not too long ago I participated in a week-long silent retreat at Elat Chayyim, a meditation center near the Catskills in New York State. I was not sure I could maintain silence for that long, but within just a short time I fell in love with being quiet. Without the need to speak, I found myself without the need of a story. At first I continued to replay my self-made and self-making tales in my mind, but after two days of silence, even these faded away. Then, for the next few days, I was nobody in particular. I was not a character in anybody's drama. I just *was*.

In those moments of just being alive, I fell into a sea of deep joy unlike anything I experience during my everyday storied life. There was nothing to defend, nothing to attack, nothing to compare myself against—because there was no self against which to make a comparison. Without all these distractions, I encountered joy, tranquility, and a sense of the inter-connectedness of all things in, with, and as God, the Source and Substance of all reality.

This joy is what Solomon points to when he tells us that everything is empty of permanence. He is not despairing but rejoicing. He is not decrying the absence of permanence but celebrating it. He knows that without the need to inflict a permanent self upon the world, without the need to invent and defend a particular story, we are capable of being in the world in a wholly different fashion. Ecclesiastes is not an attack on life's vanities and meaninglessness, but a guidebook to its deepest joys and truths.

PURSUIT OF PROFIT

When you are deluded by the illusion of permanence,
you become trapped in the pursuit of profit.
Profit for the body—wealth.
Profit for the mind—knowledge.
Profit for the soul—eternal life.
Vanity and foolishness!
Profit requires permanence, and there is no permanence.
Therefore, there is no profit, and the pursuit of profit yields only
    suffering.

from 1:3–4

The pursuit of profit makes life a means to an end rather than an end in itself. We do what we do not because of any intrinsic value or joy our actions may contain, but because we imagine that this doing will secure for us some profit in the future. Ultimately, the profit we seek is permanence, personal immortality. We are convinced that permanence is possible and that it is the source of all joy and value.

Solomon tells us that just the opposite is true. There is no permanence in the world, and the pursuit of it distracts us from being fully present to the moment. There is nothing other than here and now; and when we are distracted from this moment, we are lost to life's intrinsic meaning, value, and joy—treasures that are present only in this moment.

Periodically I am asked to lecture at an evening program for teens. During one such talk, a tall young woman about sixteen years of age stood up and said, "My best friend is dying of cancer. I need to know what happens after you die."

It was not a question; it was an urgent request. This was no time for hedging, no time for "Different people believe different things about the afterlife." She did not ask me what I *believe* happens after we die; she wanted to know what *really* happens.

The class was silent. The young woman sat down, and everyone looked at me expectantly.

"I'm sure you've all heard many things from many people about what happens after you die. I'm positive that in this room different people hold different beliefs about what happens. I won't engage in a debate over this, nor will I share abstract ideas with you. I'll tell you what I *know*. I'll tell you what I know from years of meditation and years of being with people as they die. This is what I know: you *don't* die."

I waited while this notion sank in. Then I continued: "Of course, your friend will die in the sense that she will no longer be present to you as she is now. But the friend you see when you look upon her and the self you see when you look in a mirror aren't who we really are. All people crave the security of knowing that the separate selves we perceive ourselves to be will live on in some distinct, recognizable form, and yet we aren't really those separate selves. If you want to understand what happens when you die, you have to understand who you really are right now and forever."

Who are we? We are God. And God is the whole of reality. Just as the ocean manifests as waves, so God lives as us. Just as a wave is nothing but the ocean extended in time and space, so we are nothing other than God present here and now. Just as the wave, when it dies, when it loses form, returns to its true state as the ocean, so we return to our true state as God.

Death is a waking up to the reality of who we really are. There is a moment as death overtakes us when the ego, the self we imagine our self to be, becomes so weak that it can no longer block the knowledge of our true self. The ego is still alive, but it is open to the truth that it is simply a part of God. At that moment—and I am speaking here from experience, having sensed this in meditation and having been present at the death of many people over the years—there is a deep joy that is impossible to describe.

"I'm not saying death isn't sad," I told the group. "But the sadness is for those of us who must bear the loss of someone we love. Your friend, for all the pain and suffering she may be experiencing at the moment, will find this joy. It's the way things are."

I do not know if this answer satisfied the young woman or not. Before she had a chance to respond, another student asked, "If death is so great, why not just commit suicide?"

Death comes in its own time; there is no need to rush it. Furthermore, there is no need to die physically in order to taste the joy of becoming one with God. All we need to do is meditate. In this way we can discover our true identity as God and find that liberating joy in the midst of our everyday lives.

There is a way to see through the idea of the separate ego. There is a way to free ourselves from the illusion of the immortal self and the compulsive need to protect it against discovering its own transience. All we must do is look honestly into the nature of things—their coming and going, their impermanence. If we truly understand that nothing is forever and that nothing is separate from the One, we are free from having to delude ourselves into believing the impossible. And without the need for delusion, we are free to celebrate life as it is and channel all that newly liberated energy into living life with joy.

HUNGER FOR PERMANENCE

You suffer because you hunger for permanence
and there is only impermanence.
One generation arising from the dust of another,
only to collapse itself in the heap of history.
Even the earth is passing away;
its permanence is an illusion—it passes more slowly than you,
and you mistake its slow death for eternity.
Eternity is not the infinite stretching of time, but the ending of
    time.

from 1:3–4

There are two kinds of suffering in the world: necessary and unnecessary. Necessary suffering results from those acts of nature that bring on old age, accident, illness, and death. There is nothing we can do to avoid having such natural acts happen to us and to people we love. Yet we instinctively know how to handle necessary suffering. We cry; we grieve; we move on. Unnecessary suffering poses a different kind of problem.

Let me share a story that illustrates both forms of suffering. I once worked with a family whose young child was dying. She had contracted a rare and terminal illness, and there was no hope for a cure. This sad reality was the cause of some very real suffering for all concerned. Yet for all the pain, this was a natural suffering arising out of a family's love for its daughter. She would die, they would grieve, and somehow they would find the courage and strength to move on.

The parents' best friends, however, could not accept the naturalness of the little girl's illness. The story they told themselves about life insisted that nothing happens by chance, that whatever befalls us is the result of some action of our own, either in this life or in a past life. They decided that this little girl must have committed some horrible crime in a previous life that she was being punished for in this life. They further decided that the parents of this little girl must also be guilty of some terrible offense to have given birth to a child so gravely ill. In self-defense, they cut themselves off from the family and refused to let their daughter, who was the dying girl's best friend, visit the little girl during her final weeks of life.

The suffering family lost their best friends over a story. That additional suffering was unnecessary, arising not out of the facts of life but out of the narrative their friends told themselves about the meaning of life—a narrative that is all too familiar. Solomon tells us to let our stories go and allow ourselves to become more present to life as it really is.

Although startling, this story of needless suffering is not unique. I once sat with a family in their home following the funeral of their teenage son. A neighbor dropped by to offer condolences. The dead boy's mother suddenly looked up into the face of her neighbor and screamed, "Why my son? Why my boy? He was so good!" The neighbor, apparently filled with compassion and unruffled by the mother's cry, knelt in front of her and softly said, "He must have been a murderer in a past life and this is his punishment in this life." For a second I could not breathe. Horrified, I watched as the woman collapsed in wracking sobs. Her husband, having not heard what the neighbor had said, smiled at him sadly and put an arm around his wife. I helped the neighbor to stand and walked him over to the food.

For all the needless pain he had caused this woman, he could not see beyond his story. It worked for him. "See," he was saying to her, "there is a plan and a purpose. God is in charge. Take comfort in that." She could not, and neither can I.

Yet these are the stories we tell ourselves. When a baby dies, someone almost always says, "God needed her." Or "Such an angel belongs in heaven." Or "She was too holy for this world."

Such stories help those who tell them, but they add to the suffering of those for whom they are the wrong stories. Eventually the grieving mother of the dead teenager will write her own story: she will turn to God or turn to chaos; she will project order on the world or she will find some comfort in nature's capriciousness. She will tell herself something, and that something will be added to the tale she tells herself and others in her attempt to make sense of her life.

This is human nature. It is not wrong; it is part of what we do—but not the *whole* of what we do.

To the extent that we tell stories to escape reality, we open ourselves to needless suffering and most likely inflict suffering on others. To the extent that we can see that we are by nature storytellers, and that our stories are *just* stories, we free ourselves from those stories and no longer feel compelled to defend them.

Solomon's argument is not with the fact that we tell stories. He too recognizes that this is part of human nature. His argument is with our insistence that our particular story is true. Rather than look and see what is real, as Solomon has done, we hide behind our stories and insist that they are right without daring to investigate the truth for ourselves.

When we follow Solomon's lead and investigate the nature of things for ourselves, we see the transience of all things. We see that there is nothing permanent and nothing certain. We see that chance and randomness are part of the greater order of creation. We see that all of our schemes and dreams are rooted in nothing more than a need to imagine that we are in control, that we can get what we want and hold on to it forever.

Knowing this does not put an end to our story. It simply puts an end to our *entrapment* in our story. When we are no longer entrapped in our story, we are free to encounter life as it is without having to fit it into a prefabricated schema. When there is suffering, we suffer, but we do not cling to suffering. When there is joy, we are joyous, but we do not cling to joy. Living in and for our story removes us from life. Recognizing our story for what it is—a story and not reality—allows us to accept that part of our nature even as we embrace the greater reality that our story seeks to deny.

THE SEA IS NEVER FULL

The sun climbs eagerly through the sky only to tumble into
    darkness.
It crawls through the night and returns to the climb only to fall
    once more.
The wind blows south, then north;
round upon round of endless spinning.
Rivers pour tirelessly into the sea, and yet the sea is never full.

There is no purpose to it.
Sun, wind, river act according to their nature;
they do what they do because of what they are.
Only you insist upon meaning and purpose.
For you the Way is not enough; for you it must be a Way To
when in fact it is only the Way Of.

from 1:5–8

It is because of passages such as this that people often misread
Ecclesiastes as a melancholy book. They imagine that Solomon
is saying life is pointless: the sun rises and sets only to rise again;
the rivers pour into the ocean and never fill it up. There is no end
to life's routine—and no point. But that is not what Ecclesiastes
is saying. Rather than bemoan the round of life, Solomon
celebrates it.

The point of life, he says, is life itself. Life does not *have* a point;
it *is* the point. The sun rising—how marvelous! The sun
setting—how wonderful! The rivers flowing—how delicious!
Everything acting according to its nature is the very point of
existence.

This should be enough for us, Solomon says, but it is not; we
want more. We want life to lead to something beyond itself. We

approach life as a means to something else, and as long as we are focused on this something else, we fail to tap the simple wonder of what is happening right here and now: the rising and setting of the sun, the gurgle of a baby, the cry of a friend seeking a shoulder to lean on. Our desire for something else distracts us from the real source of joy in our lives, and that is why we are so often needlessly melancholy.

This passage of Ecclesiastes reminds me of the Greek myth of Sisyphus. Sisyphus is doomed by the gods to push a huge boulder up a mountain, only to have it slip back down to the bottom, where he starts to push it up toward the summit all over again. When I first heard this myth in high school, I assumed with my fellow students that this was a metaphor for hell. Maybe so, but when I look at this myth as I approach the half-century mark in my journey, I see it as an apt description of most of my life. And my life is not hellish at all.

This morning I unloaded the dishwasher. In a few days I will have to do it again. Right now I can hear the washing machine whirring through its spin cycle. My clothes will be clean for a while, and then I will have to wash them again. Each week I write a sermon and lead my congregation in religious services, only to start preparing all over again for the following week. It may not be a boulder I am pushing, but my life is no less repetitive than that of Sisyphus.

I suspect what is true of my life is true of most lives. We all do dishes and wash clothes. We vacuum the same floors over and over again. We shop for food over and over again. We keep going to bed at night and getting up in the morning, only to go to bed the next night and get up the next morning. We are all Sisyphus.

Is this hell? Is this a matter for despair? My high school teacher may have thought so, but I no longer do. I like clean clothes, so I wash them. The fact that they get dirty again does not bother me in the least. The same is true with vacuuming, shopping, going to sleep, waking up, and doing my job. The only way these actions could be hell is if I thought doing any of them should be a once-and-for-all proposition. If I thought that I should have to wash my clothes only once and that they should stay clean forever, then I would be depressed at their failure to live up to that expectation. But I do not think this. I know better.

Solomon wants us to know better about all of life. It is not a matter of one sunrise and one sunset; the sun rises and sets and rises and sets in a never-ending round of beauty. It is not the cycle that is the problem, but our refusal to appreciate the wonder of it.

The sun does not complain about rising and setting. The river never despairs over failing to fill the sea. Only you and I do this. Only you and I insist upon something other than now, something more valuable than here and the actions we engage in presently. Only you and I are so trapped in the future that we disparage the present.

Solomon is not bemoaning the goallessness of sunrise; he is celebrating it. He is holding it up as a model for us: do what you do without thought of reward; do what you do in a manner that honors the doing without getting trapped in where it may be going.

PASSION FOR PURPOSE

Your passion for purpose traps you in the pursuit of
    permanence.
Your hunger for meaning blinds you to the simple beauty of the
    turnings.
There is no tranquility in the Way To;
yet the Way Of is peace itself.

from 1:5–8

We want life to lead to something beyond itself. We want to believe that we are here on this earth for a purpose that transcends merely being here. We imagine that we are here to do something special, to achieve some purpose or goal that is greater than the everyday encounters of our ordinary lives. Life is a "way to" rather than a "way of."

Solomon tells us that life's value is intrinsic to life itself. The value of living is living. Life does not point to anything beyond itself. Life needs nothing else to make it worthwhile; it is worthwhile in and of itself. As long as we insist that life is *for* something else, we will focus our energies on that something else. And when we fail to get it—and we *will* fail, since this something else is a story of our making and not real in itself—we will despair of life.

Real despair comes not from Solomon's bold investigation into life's impermanence but from our own insistence that life be something it is not. Yet when we recognize, as Solomon does, that life is valuable just as it is, that life is a Way Of achieving peace rather than the Way To peace, we are suddenly filled with a joy that surpasses verbal articulation.

I have a friend who teaches little children to play the violin. I once asked her how she gets the children to practice. "Oh, we never practice," she said, "we just play."

She teaches her students how to play the violin and to find joy in their playing. At first they may play poorly, while later they may play well—but poorly or well, they are always playing the violin. The joy of playing is present from the beginning. They are not *learning how to play* in order to someday play and then find the joy that comes with playing. They are *playing* from the start—just not as well as they will play after years of playing. No practice, just play. Practice is the Way To; playing is the Way Of.

The Way To projects joy into the future. The Way Of makes joy an integral part of the present. Solomon is suggesting that when we live life as it is rather than as we wish it to be, when we live without getting trapped in our stories, we will find life to be intrinsically joyous and peaceful. This does not mean that we will not make mistakes or encounter pain and suffering. This only means that without our story to distract us, we will encounter pain and suffering as part of the play and in that way learn to accept it without the added grief of having to fit it into some greater drama.

I SOUGHT ORDER

I sought order and found only chaos.
I sought the straight and found only crookedness.
I sought solace and found only suffering. . . .

Thus do I teach:
The more you seek security, the more you are haunted by
    insecurity.
The more you desire surety, the more you are plagued by
    change.
The more you pretend to permanence, the more you invite
    suffering.
The more you do for control, the less you do for joy.

from 1:15–18

It seems we have the whole of life exactly backward. We want what we cannot get, and we reject that which we have in abundance. We want the world to fit into a neat and understandable package. What we get is a jumble of experiences from which we fashion a life. We want life to fit our story about life. Instead, we find ourselves in a swirling soup of ever-changing events, some of which seem to make no sense whatsoever.

So Solomon is correct: the more I crave security, the more I am haunted by its absence. The more I seek to maintain the status quo, no matter how hurtful or damaging to me and others, the more things slip through my fingers and change against my will. Indeed—and this is his main point—my will does not much matter. Things happen whether I will them to or not. Reality does not give a damn about what I want; it just does what it does.

Our task, then, is simply to be fully present to whatever is happening now. When we are fully present, we seem to know what to do. Doing becomes effortless, choiceless. We are not weighing options but simply taking up the task that the moment presents.

My friend Leon is a chaplain at a local hospital. We cover for each other when one of us is out of town. Late one evening I got a call from his hospital about a family whose mother was dying. Leon was unavailable, and they asked me to drive to the hospital and help in any way I could.

When I arrived at the hospital, the woman had just died and the family was being ushered out of her room by an orderly. I asked the family if they had had a chance to pray with their mother and say good-bye. They had not, and the orderly was kind enough to let us back into their mother's room to be with her for a while longer.

I encouraged the family to gather around their mother and take turns speaking to her—telling her they loved her, that they would miss her, and that though it was sad, it was okay that it was her time to die. As they spoke to their mother, the dead woman's eyes suddenly filled with blood, and thick red tears began to stream down her cheeks. I had never seen this happen to anyone before, and neither had her family. They stopped talking and just stared, their bodies tense.

Part of me was horrified. I had performed this kind of service for people many times, and this had never happened before. If I had thought about what to do, I suspect I would have left the room and called for a nurse. But I did not think about it. Instead, I sat on the bed, took the woman's head in my arms, and wiped away the blood with a towel that had been hanging on the bedrail. I nodded to the family and encouraged them to continue speaking to her. I did all of this as if it were the most natural thing in the world. And at the time, it was. After I left the hospital and returned to my car, however, I began shaking all over.

I still feel that I did the right thing, and I learned something in the process. The lesson I learned was not simply what to do in this particular situation; rather, I learned the wisdom that comes when we are simply present. I did not have a set procedure to handle the situation we faced. In fact, it was not a "situation" that needed handling. It was simply a family grieving, a mother bleeding, and a rabbi with access to a towel.

This is what I mean by being present to the moment. Nothing magical or extraordinary, just life as it is—often messy and rarely scripted. The more I empty myself of self and of the quest for surety, permanence, and control that defines the self, the more I am at home in the chaos of my life. The less we imagine what our lives ought to be, the more we can be present to what they really are. And in this there is a grace—an ease of doing—that we cannot imagine as long as we seek to control and manipulate things to meet our ends.

PLEASURE

So I said to myself:
Perhaps it is only wisdom that is folly.
Perhaps in pleasure there is a greater truth and certainty.

But pleasure proved to be no more solid than wisdom;
the body no more stable than the mind.
Laughter is as fleeting as insight,
and joy no more permanent than profit.
Pleasure, no less than knowledge, is fundamentally empty;
and both are without meaning if by meaning we seek
    permanence.

from 2:1–7

Solomon was an explorer of the human condition. He was not a forest-dwelling monk but a lusty king with the cash to try whatever struck his fancy. If the pursuit of wisdom failed to bring him solace, perhaps the search for pleasure would.

Solomon drank, gambled, had nine hundred wives, and exploited every sensual pleasure imaginable—all for science, you understand—and still found no lasting joy. Why? Because *nothing* lasts.

Whenever we use pleasure to mask the unnecessary suffering of life that we generate for ourselves by insisting upon permanence, we end up right back where we started. And over time, we need more and more doses of pleasure to combat deeper and deeper bouts of suffering. There is no end to it.

The key to living well is remembering that nothing lasts. Holding that key, we simply respond honestly and cleanly to whatever comes our way. We do not fear suffering when it comes, because we know that it cannot last. We do not dampen our joy by worrying whether or not it will end; we know it will end and thus hold it all the more precious. When we hurt or are sad or depressed, we simply live out those sensations. They will pass. Everything does.

It is our insistence on permanence that is the source of all our unnecessary fear and suffering. Because we believe in permanence, we worry that the suffering we feel now will last forever. Rather than allow it to play itself out and move on, we focus on it and seek to cure it, to alleviate it. We use all kinds of drugs and distractions to make the suffering go away, when in fact it *will* go away of its own accord (and the distractions only add to our pain and dis-ease). Likewise, because we believe in permanence, we want to stretch a moment of joy into eternity. We want it to last. We try to freeze the joy, horde it, ration it so it will last forever. But all we really succeed in doing is replacing true joy with anxiety about joy.

Nothing lasts, Solomon tells us, and that is the most liberating truth of all.

We can check this out for ourselves by observing our mental state dispassionately. If we look carefully, we will see that there is no steady-state emotion. We are happy for a moment and then not happy for a moment. We are anxious for a moment and then not anxious for a moment. We may prefer some feelings to others, but we are open to all of them. We may seek to hold on to those feelings we like and avoid those we do not like, but like them or not, they just keep coming and going.

Sometimes in my seminars I invite people to imagine the following scenario: You wake up in the morning anxious over a meeting you have scheduled for later in the day. As you shower, you suddenly have a brainstorm and know exactly what to say at the meeting. Excitement replaces depression. As you drive to your meeting, a song comes on the radio that reminds you of a recently lost love. Sadness replaces excitement. Right in the middle of the song an eighteen-wheeler nearly runs you off the road. Fear and then relief and then anger push excitement, and then each other, out of your mind. When you arrive at your meeting, you cannot find a convenient parking space. Frustration replaces anger. As you climb out of your car, you notice a glimmer between the driver's seat and the utility console; reaching down, you find the expensive piece of jewelry you lost last week. Joy replaces frustration. By this point in the scenario, most people have gotten the idea: there is no steady-state emotion, just one feeling after another.

When we understand this on a very personal level, we are free to feel whatever we feel without fear that it will last (in the case of suffering or other negative emotions) or the anxiety that it will leave (in the case of joy or other positive emotions). Suffering will pass, and joy will pass; and over time both will return and leave and return and leave over and over again. We do not have to avoid suffering to be free from it. It will pass of its own accord. We do not have to horde joy to be present to it. It will come again of its own accord. We have only to appreciate each moment for what it is while it is.

A man came to see me recently, complaining of an overwhelming sense of guilt. His father had died within the past two months and he was following the Jewish rituals that deal with grief. After the traditional month of mourning, he chose to go to a movie—a highly rated comedy—with a friend. He felt uneasy about going (after all, his father had just died), and he really did not feel that a comedy was appropriate—but at his friend's insistence he went.

As the previews of coming attractions droned on, he could not shake his guilt over being in the theater. He decided to leave, but then the film started, and he felt he could not walk out on his friend. So he sat and watched. Soon he was lost in the story. Then he laughed. The movie was funny and he *laughed*. For a moment he forgot about his father and just enjoyed the antics on the screen. Life was good.

Then he remembered his dad. How could he be laughing at a time like this? What kind of awful, callous son had he turned out to be? How could he find forgiveness for such a stupid act?

All of this angst is unnecessary, a drama overlaid on the simple fact that he laughed. In other words, he responded appropriately to what was happening at the moment—something funny happened on the screen and he laughed—and then appropriately again when the moment passed and his sad thoughts of his father returned. In order to make sense of the juxtaposition of moments, he concocted a self-castigating story that made his laughter inappropriate. According to this story, the reason he laughed was not because the movie was funny but that he was a bad son. The *real* problem, however, was neither his laughing nor his sadness; it was his need to link the two of them in some coherent way. In seeking to create a story that would tie everything together, all he could come up with was a tale that cast him as the villain. The result was needless depression and guilt.

The fact is there is no coherent story implicit in life. There is just life. We are sad. We are silly. We are neutral. We are angry. We are horny. We are happy. We have a full range of feelings that come and go—none lasting, none good or bad, and none the essence of who we are.

The madness of life never drives us insane. It is the insane desire for coherence that drives us mad.

DESIRE

Whatever I desired I took.
I denied myself nothing, and I rejoiced in all I had.
Yes, rejoiced!
Do not pretend there is no joy in ownership or pleasure.
Do not mistake me for one who denies the flesh.
For such is the way of the fool who has nothing and so denies
       desire.
There is desire, and there is pleasure in achieving one's desire.
But there is no permanence.

Pleasure no less than knowledge is empty of permanence
and is thus unable to bring the gift of tranquility.

from 2:8–10

Solomon is not an ascetic refusing to take pleasure in the good things of life; he simply understands that satisfying the desires of the flesh serves our quest for permanence no better than satisfying any other desires. Solomon's experiment is to see if there is anything in the world that will satisfy our craving for permanence. His conclusion is that there is not. Nothing lasts, and as long as we desire permanence above all else, we will be disappointed.

Everything that we encounter is a temporary manifestation of life. Everything comes and everything goes away. Anticipating the first and grieving over the second will do nothing to change this fact. And according to Solomon, there is no *need* to change it. All we need do is *accept* it. Solomon tells us that the world is no less wondrous for its being temporary. But if we are not willing to accept its fleeting nature, we will be incapable of fully appreciating what it has to offer. When we focus on what life is not, we cannot take delight in what life is.

What Ecclesiastes tells us is this: the past and the future are out of our control, and the present is impermanent and fleeting. If we are going to find joy in life, we cannot find it in the past or the future. We must find it here and now, in the present. And since the present is impermanent, we have to be fully attentive to it if we are to appreciate it at all. If we are daydreaming about tomorrow or agonizing over yesterday, we will miss whatever it is today has to offer. Life is here and now. We must pay attention to it. We must learn what we can from each encounter and, when appropriate, apply that knowledge to the next. We can plan for the future, but we must not expect the future to conform to our plan. We can learn from the past, but we must not expect to replicate it in the present.

Only when we taste the world as it is, respecting it for what it is and honoring its pleasures and pains as they come and go—only then can we partake of the joys that this world has to offer without souring them with the self-defeating desire for permanence.

NEEDLESS SUFFERING

If you are trapped in the quest for permanence,
each day boils with anger, frustration, and needless suffering.
Night grants no rest,
and your mind seethes in rage over the theft of security.

You center your world on self;
you pamper yourself with pity;
you delude yourself with vanity—
and none of it gives you what you seek.
For your pursuit of permanence is but the ego's flight from
        truth.
The pursuit is vain,
the prize is mischief,
and in the end all you have is what you are:
emptiness upon emptiness upon emptiness.

                                            from 2:22–23

Most of us who are dealing with issues of anger are really
dealing with lives that refuse to meet our expectations and
demands. Solomon tells us that the way out of this anger is to
realize that life does not care about what we desire. Take the self
out of the picture and respond to the reality of the moment, and
anger fades away. Not everything is wonderful and just when we
live in the moment, but even the injustices of life are best fought
without self-righteous anger.

At a recent workshop I taught, a man said, "I was coming to
this seminar this morning and a panhandler accosts me right here
in the parking lot. He wants money. Hell, we *all* want money. *I*
want money, and I work hard to earn it. So why do I have to

bother with this guy? Why should I help him out at all? And what right does he have to bother me, anyway? So not only didn't I give him any money, I chased him out of the parking lot."

The other workshop participants responded in a variety of ways to this man's story. Some were horrified that he had not helped the panhandler out. Others were overjoyed that he had stood up to the panhandler and had refused to help. A few talked about karma and how the panhandler's need to ask connected with the other man's need to give.

After people had discussed this for a few moments, I said to the man, "You really felt that this panhandler was out to get you personally, didn't you?"

"Damn right I did. And he was. He spotted me parking my BMW. He knew I had money and he wanted some of it."

"Did he ask anyone else for money?" I asked.

"Sure. He asked everyone coming in here, I guess."

"Then why do you imagine he was singling you out? Why do you assume you're so special to this man? If he was asking everyone, why focus on yourself?"

When we imagine that life is aimed at us, we become trapped in our sense of self. We somehow feel that we are the target of God's anger or largesse. This is certainly not what Solomon teaches us. He reminds us that we are not the target. There *is* no target. There is just life happening here and now—sometimes pleasant, sometimes unpleasant; sometimes in accord with our desires, sometimes not in accord with our desires.

When we imagine that we are special, that life is targeting us, then we put ourselves at the center of a drama and react with anger when things do not go our way. When we realize that we are not the target, we can deal with life without the added pain and anger of imagining that we are being singled out.

I know a woman in my congregation who has breast cancer. She is, unfortunately, one of many in my community who deal with this disease. As I sat with her at a charity luncheon for cancer research, I was amazed to hear how she answered a query from another woman at our table.

"Why do you think God chose to give you breast cancer?" the woman asked.

"I don't think God chooses such things," my friend said.

"Well, you must have done something to attract the cancer to you. I mean, we *are* responsible for what happens to us. We choose our own reality, you know."

"No, I don't know that at all. We're responsible for how we handle what life brings, not the things it brings. We don't choose our reality, only how we respond to reality."

"Well," the other woman continued, "I read that it's anger that weakens the immune system and that only the most angry people get cancer. Maybe you should do something about your anger."

"I'm not an especially angry person," my friend said. "Nor do I think that anger is the key to cancer. Cancer isn't the physical expression of repressed or expressed rage. While our emotions may certainly impact our immune systems, there are too many other factors—especially environmental factors brought on by pollution and the use of toxic chemicals in so many aspects of our lives—to say that cancer is caused by any one factor, especially an emotional one."

I do not know how the other woman would have responded to my friend's remarks, because I could not contain myself any longer.

"Why," I asked her, "do you feel this ungodly need to blame the patient for the disease? Why can't it just be that cancer happens? Why isn't that enough for you?"

The woman just looked at me and said nothing. I used her silence as an excuse to continue.

"I suspect you have to blame people because you need to

assure yourself that you won't get cancer. I think that what you're seeking is a reason for cancer that exempts you from having to worry about getting sick. I think that you're totally unconcerned with other people or their health, and totally fixated on yourself and your health. Your questions show no compassion for people with cancer, only an obsession with yourself."

I probably could have gone on for another few minutes if the woman had not stood up and walked away.

I turned to my companion, expecting a smile of solidarity. Instead, she stared at me in amazement.

"What was *that* all about?" she asked.

"What do you mean?" I said. "That woman was obnoxious. Weren't you bothered by what she said?"

"No. She was just talking. I didn't take any of it personally."

"What do you mean you didn't take it personally? You have cancer. She was talking about you and why you have cancer. It doesn't get more personal than that. She was *attacking* you! Why aren't you angry and upset?"

"You're wrong," she said as she returned to her meal. "She wasn't talking to me or about me. She was just working out her own ideas and fears. I didn't put myself in this at all. I just listened to what she had to say and responded from what I know to be true. I didn't feel attacked at all."

My companion's reaction is what it means to live without being the target. We can be very effective without getting angry. She shows how effectively we can respond to difficult circumstances in the absence of anger, and how personally we can respond to hostility if we refrain from taking things personally.

APPRECIATING ALL THAT
COMES YOUR WAY

There is no other good than
eating when hungry,
drinking when thirsty,
and appreciating all that comes your way.
For pleasure and profit are empty as the wind;
there is no lasting joy at all.
Joy is as fleeting as the breeze.
Celebrate its coming, and do not seek to halt its passing
       away.

from 2:24

We make life so complicated, and then we use complexity as our excuse for living life poorly. This passage from Ecclesiastes suggests that life is really quite simple. It is eating. It is drinking. It is appreciating.

Can that really be the case? What about love? What about career? What about success? What about money?

Solomon does not deny these things; indeed, he pursues them with gusto. Yet what he finds is that there is only the *pursuit*. Grasping and attaining any of these things permanently is impossible. Love, satisfaction, and wealth all come and go. That is their nature. That is the nature of everything—to come and to go. All Solomon is saying is that when they come, be happy. When they go, be sad. Do not add to this by concocting a grand drama about why things are the way they are.

A friend of mine invited me to sit in on a discussion group he was facilitating on the topic of fear. A man in his middle twenties opened the discussion by saying that his major fear was not having enough money.

"Why is that your major fear?" my friend asked.

"Because whenever I don't have enough money, I feel out of control."

My friend looked thoughtful. "But why does a lack of money lead to a sense of being out of control?" he asked.

"Because when I was a teenager, my family went through some hard times, and I couldn't do what my friends were doing."

"Why else might you equate money and control?" my friend asked.

"Well, when I was eight years old, my dad lost his job."

My friend pressed on: "Why does your dad's losing his job impact your sense of control?"

"Because I know he had dreams for all of us—dreams that he couldn't fulfill. He couldn't afford them."

"So your *father* felt out of control when he lacked money," my friend said, clarifying.

"Right."

"So why are you feeling what your father felt?" my friend asked, still pursuing the elusive *why*.

"Oh, because when I was six . . . "

Others in the group jumped into the conversation, and we explored this man's issues for another five or ten minutes. In the end, we had helped him construct a fascinating story about how he had internalized his father's fears and was living out his father's issues as if they were his own.

It was a good story, but I could not shake the nagging suspicion that that was *all* it was: just a good story. The man seemed to find the discussion meaningful, my friend gave him lots of encouragement to embellish his tale, and the rest of the group appeared riveted to his every word. But in the end, I still felt that it was just a story.

After the class ended, I asked the man how discovering his story about money and control would change his life.

"Well," he said without a moment's hesitation, "now I know why I feel the way I do."

"And how will knowing change things for you?" I asked.

"I don't know," he said, smiling, "but it will."

I hope he is right. But I wonder if his story will not now become the focus of his attention, drawing energy away from doing what he needs to do to secure his financial well-being.

Reality is reality, regardless of our story. Lack of money is scary to this man. Fine. I suspect that he is not unique in this. But I would ask him not why he fears poverty but what he is going to do to improve his chances of never being poor. Fear itself is not a problem; it is what we do with fear that can be a problem.

When fear brings something to our attention and we respond by reducing the danger of the situation, then fear is helpful. When fear becomes our focal point, when our aim is to fix the fear rather than face the situation, then fear is a distraction.

This is what Solomon is trying to tell us. Life continually presents us with challenging situations, and we typically respond by hiding behind distractions. Caught up in a secondary struggle with our ideas about what is happening, and why, we lose sight of what is *really* happening. Better to simply accept reality for what it is and then make of it what we can.

MOMENTS

Life is fleeting,
the passing of moments upon moments.
Embrace them as they come;
do not cling to them as they go.
In this alone is there tranquility.
Moments of birth, moments of death;
moments of planting, moments of uprooting;
moments of killing, moments of healing;
moments of knocking down, moments of building up;
moments of mourning, moments of dancing;
moments of casting stones, moments of gathering stones;
moments of embracing, moments of departing;
moments of seeking, moments of forsaking;
moments of keeping, moments of discarding;
moments of tearing, moments of mending;
moments of silence, moments of speech;
moments of love, moments of hate;
moments of war, moments of peace.
Moments and the passing of moments—this is life.

from 3:1–9

Life is a series of moments. And the only moment of which we can be aware is this moment right now. Even when we conjure up memories of the past or fantasize about the future, we are conjuring and fantasizing in the present. There is only now, and now, and now again. I find this endlessly liberating. Not everyone does, however.

One of my teachers in rabbinical school taught that this passage of Ecclesiastes violated the entire sense of Western civilization by denying the importance of history and robbing us of hope for a better future. His position was that the present is the result of the past and sets the stage for the future, and that Solomon's focus on moments erases the continuity from past to future. But surely this is not what Solomon is saying at all.

Solomon's message is that moments change. While the past may impact the present, it cannot determine it. After all, how can moments of tearing lead to moments of mending? At what point does tearing become mending? Tearing may create a need for mending, but in and of itself, it cannot become mending. Tearing is always tearing. If we fixate on the past, and the past is about tearing, then where will the act of mending come into play? For mending to happen, we have to be free from the past, free in this moment to choose differently than we have in past moments.

Solomon is reminding us that each moment carries with it the chance to be something new. I may have been tearing for a long time, but at any moment I can stop tearing and start mending. I do not have to go back and fix the past; I simply have to do something new in the present. In fact, I *cannot* go back and fix the past. That is what it means to *be* past. I can take responsibility for the past and seek to do differently in the present, but I cannot pretend that my present actions can undo past behavior.

There is a wonderful Jewish proverb: "Stir a pot of filth one way or stir it another, it is always going to be a pot of filth. Better to spend our time stringing pearls for the sake of heaven." The past is past. We can look at it one way or we can look at it some other way, but in the end it is what it is, and the energy we spend on stirring it up could better be used to deal constructively with the present.

Not having to fix the past is liberating. Rather than having to channel our energy into undoing past wrongs, we can focus on doing what is right in the present. Doing what is right may mean seeking to make amends for past wrongs, but even this cannot erase those wrongs. We have to accept the past, learn from it, and eventually let it go so that we can make what we can of the present.

The key to applying this passage of Ecclesiastes to our lives is being aware of what action is called for in the moment. Solomon sets forth a wide range of opposites. There is a time to scatter stones and a time to gather them together. There is a time to throw things away and a time to keep them close. There is a time for war and a time for peace.

He is not saying that we should only make peace, or only hold on to things, or only gather things together. He is saying that the whole gamut of human options is available to us, and the challenge is to know which option is appropriate here and now in this very situation. Life is this moment, and this moment, and this moment. No matter how similar one moment may be to a million others, still it is not any of them. It is itself. It is now. It is new. And it requires a fresh response.

ETERNITY

The matter of suffering is clear to me:
it arises from ignorance of impermanence.
Everything functions in time;
everything flows, changes, transforms.
In your heart you sense eternity,
but your mind mistakes it for time without end.
Eternity is not endless time;
eternity is the ending of time.
Under the sun it is all flux and flow,
diverse and separate.
But under the sun is not the whole, and
there is a deeper truth
embracing the many in a greater One.

3:10–11

The world that you and I know, the world we experience when we experience ourselves as separate beings, is a world of time, a world of impermanence—what Solomon calls the world under the sun. Solomon hints, however, that there is another world— or rather, another way of *looking* at the world—a way that Solomon calls the heart's sense of eternity.

We have to look carefully at this idea of eternity if we are to understand what Ecclesiastes is saying. If we take eternity to mean time without end, we mistake it for permanence; and permanence does not exist. Eternity is not time without end but an ending of time. Both permanence and impermanence depend upon time: the former seeks to freeze it, the latter seeks to let it flow, but both focus on it. What Ecclesiastes is saying is that there is some reality that is not dependent upon time, and we have an intuitive understanding of this timeless reality implanted within us.

Most of us have experienced this timeless realm. Some call it being in the Zone; others refer to it as Flow. However we might name it, it is a sense of time stopping. When we are in Flow or in the Zone, we are so absorbed in the present that we drop all concern with self, time, and eternity. There is just now, and now never ends.

This happens to me most often during moments of meditation. While it is difficult to find language that accurately describes such moments, I have had the experience of being fully present during meditation, with no sense of time passing at all. At such moments, my sense of self fades away. My focus on my breathing becomes simply breathing, without any sense of *my*. I am not asleep then, or lost in thought. On the contrary, I have an acute sense of the world, but there is at the same time no *I* that is doing the sensing. And when the *I* returns, I discover that thirty minutes have passed in what seems to be no time at all—literally.

Once when I spoke of this experience at a meditation retreat in Ann Arbor, Michigan, a woman commented that she often had the same kind of experience while doing needlepoint. Working on her needlepoint, her attention would be so focused as to put an end to everything else. She would follow the needlepoint pattern flawlessly, yet without a sense of *herself* doing the work at all—just the work, just the needle going in and out of the stretched cloth. This demanding work would happen, from her point of view, without any sense of effort, self, or the passing of time.

What is the value of these timeless moments? When we return from such a moment, we feel lighter, more open, more connected to others. It is as if someone had taken the hard shell of our ego and perforated it to let in the rest of the world. We are filled with a quiet joy that can stay with us for quite some time.

Solomon reminds us that we each have this capacity to open to eternity, not as an immortal self living in some time without end, but through the ending of self and time by becoming one with the immediacy of the moment. The key is to find a practice that creates the focused attention that is so central to the ending of our sense of separate self.

Meditation is one such practice; needlepoint is another. Indeed, anything that we do with full attention can be a doorway into the timeless world above the sun. I would recommend that you find a practice and master it. But I would also caution that you not seek to use this practice to escape the ordinary world of self and time. Ecclesiastes is a celebration of this world, not a call to abandon it. While it is helpful to experience the timeless world of Flow, the real value in doing so is in returning to the timely world of fleeting moments with a deeper sense of tranquility and peace.

THE SIMPLE TRUTH

Thus I understand the simple truth of life:
there is nothing better than for you to rejoice
in every deed done in harmony with the moment.
For doing is your purpose;
in doing is your meaning.
Leave the result to those who come after you,
and attend solely to doing well that which must be done at all.

from 3:21–22

Doing in harmony with the moment is Ecclesiastes' key to tranquility. Solomon has already told us that each moment has its own integrity: a moment for birth, a moment for death, and so on. Our challenge is to discern the integrity of the moment and act in sync with it.

We tend to act not in harmony with the moment but in harmony with our own story about the moment—a story arising from our need for coherence and permanence over and above whatever intrinsic value the moment itself may carry. We project our need for permanence onto the moment and act from that, when what we really need to do is let go of our projections and stories and perceive what the moment calls forth in and of itself.

How do we do this? I suggest the practice of meditation: sitting quietly for thirty to forty minutes once or twice a day and just observing what happens. There are many systems of meditation to choose from, but the aim with regard to Ecclesiastes is the same: to observe the fundamental impermanence of self.

We tend to identify with our feelings, our thoughts, our aches and pains. Yet none of these stays around long enough to provide a solid basis for a permanent sense of self. In fact, I would suggest that while we may say that we are identifying with thoughts and feelings, what we are *really* doing is identifying with an imaginary self that is having these thoughts and feelings.

When I sit in meditation and observe the workings of my body/mind, I cannot find anything permanent. My thoughts, feelings, and physical sensations are speeding into and out of awareness. There is nothing to hold on to, nothing to point to and say, "That is me." Yet I need just that sense of permanent self in order to maintain my view of the world as a stable place. So I imagine that behind all these sensations there is an immaterial, incorporeal, and immortal *me* that lives forever, first in this world and then in the world to come.

Yet this self is no more permanent than the sensations it is supposed to be sensing. Try this experiment: Right now, as you read these words, ask yourself, Who is reading this book? The fact that you know that *you* are reading suggests that the *you* who is reading is not the *you* who knows you are reading. Maybe that second *you* is the real *you*, the birthless and deathless *you*.

Now ask yourself this question: Who is aware of the *you* that is aware of the *you* that is reading this book? The fact that you know that you are aware of yourself reading suggests that there is a *you* behind the knowing *you* who is aware of both the knowing *you* and the reading *you*. Perhaps *this you* is the real *you*, the birthless and deathless *you*.

This exercise could go on indefinitely. We could always imagine another self who knows all the selves of which we are cumulatively aware. There is no end to it because there is no *it* toward which the game points. There is no final, end-of-the-line, the-buck-stops-here, permanent, separate self that knows all the others.

Sometimes during workshops I use an onion to illustrate this point. I pass out small onions to my students and ask them to see the onion as a metaphor for their sense of self. Then I ask them to remove one layer of onion skin at a time, imagining that each layer is a layer of self. In the end, with tears streaming down our faces, we come to the heart of the onion, the core of the self: empty space.

An onion *has* no core. It is just layer of skin upon layer of skin. There is no heart of the onion that one can point to and say, This is what the onion really is.

The same is true of the self. It is just layer upon layer of perception and sensation without a core. At the heart of it all is emptiness.

Does the emptiness of an onion make the onion meaningless or render onionhood depressive? Not at all. An onion is no less valuable for its lack of permanent self. It is no less an onion for having no core.

Does the emptiness of the self make the self meaningless or selfhood depressive? Not at all. We are no less unique, wondrous, and valuable for our lack of permanence. We are still ourselves, even if we lack a core self.

This is not the end of the exercise, however. After each layer of onion skin has been set aside, I ask people to cup in their hands what is left, to cradle a bit of the emptiness in their palms. I then ask them to share what they hold with each other and see what they have in common. Each person is cradling the same emptiness. There is no distinction between what one person is holding and what another person is holding. It is the emptiness that we all have in common.

What is true of the onion is true of the self. At its core, there is no separate self—no *I*—distinct from all others. At its core, when all the layers of self have been put aside, there is a common nothingness that all selves share. What is this universal nothingness? It is God, the One whose name is I AM.

Solomon knows that each of us is searching for a permanent *I* at the heart of who we are. He knows that no such *I* exists, however, for there is no separate thing anywhere. He knows that our search for separateness and permanence is at the root of all unnecessary suffering. Furthermore, he knows that relief from this unnecessary suffering will come when we abandon the quest and acknowledge that no such separate *I* exists. But he is *not* saying, in the above passage, that no *I* exists at all—only that the *I* that is, is the I AM that is all of us.

When the Bible tells us that God is I AM, it is letting us know that God is the true *I*, the one thing from which all things arise, in which all things rest, and to which all things return. When we strip away our layers of self, we find not selfish individuality but self*less* universality. We discover that the *I* we think we are is but a temporary manifestation of the only *I* there is: God. We are not alone and cut off from God; we are one with, in, and as God, as our own experience can attest.

When we are in touch with this truth, we are in sync with the moment and know what to do in order to live our life with integrity, justice, compassion, and peace. But as long as the quest for a separate self occupies our minds, we cannot be in tune with the moment. When we discover that we and the moment arise from the same Source, we are free from projections and ready to do, without hesitation or fear, what needs to be done.

DO WHAT YOU LOVE

Why do you labor so hard? . . .
There is nothing you can own that is not on its way to dust.
The pursuit of permanence is but chasing after wind. . . .

Your problem is not with work but with the fruits of your work.
Better one handful earned with joy than two earned with
    vexation.
Do what you love, and contentment may follow.
Do what you hate, and no amount of wealth will buy you peace.

                                            from 4:4–6

Sigmund Freud once said that the secret to life is found in love and work. Solomon might agree. Love and work can be satisfying. They can also be painful. In fact, over the course of time, each is both.

Solomon's concern is the ulterior motive that most people have regarding love and work, a hidden agenda that asks of each something that neither can provide. As long as that ulterior motive governs our actions, neither love nor work can achieve its potential. What we seek—that ulterior motive—is permanence. What we find is impermanence; and rather than make peace with reality, we double our efforts to deny it, imposing a false sense of security that just cannot hold up.

Why do we work so hard? What do we hope to gain from our labors? Over the entrance to one of their death camps, the Nazis hung a sign that read, "Work Makes Free." The Nazis knew that the slogan was a lie, yet so many of us continue to have faith in its message. Work will, we insist, make us free.

Work becomes a means to an end that cannot be achieved. And because the end is unreal and never satisfied, work becomes a kind of slavery. We labor for security, for permanence, for something that will not change or let us down. Rather than admit that our goal is unreal, we work harder and harder, hoping to mask the truth of impermanence behind the sweat and stress of our ever-increasing labor.

The magazine *Fast Company* is devoted to cutting-edge business thinking. Its tag line, a quote from Hunter Thompson, points to the heart of Ecclesiastes' warning. It reads, "Faster and faster until the thrill of speed overcomes the fear of death." The fear of death is our gnawing intuition regarding the emptiness of all things. There is nothing secure, nothing fixed, nothing permanent. "Emptiness, emptiness," cries Ecclesiastes. "Faster, faster," screams the ego. If we keep working faster, if we never stop to catch our breath, consider our fate, look clearly at what we are doing, then we can create the illusion of permanence.

But there is a limit to faster and faster. In time we tire. We have to rest. And when we do, we are overwhelmed by the rising tide of impermanence, flooded by dread over the emptiness of our lives.

The solution? Solomon advises work—but work from which we do not ask anything it cannot deliver. Work at something you love, he says, and find satisfaction in what you do. Make work intrinsically valuable. Find something to do that gives you pleasure. That way, when work ends, you will have reaped its benefits already and can let it go without regret.

The same is true of love. When a relationship ends, the couple focuses on the ending and uses the pain of loss to pollute the joy of having once been together. They project the breakup back into the past and poison the love that once blessed them. It is as if they were saying, "Since there is no love now, there could not have been love then. And if there was no love then, we were simply using each other, cheating each other, debasing each other." From this perspective comes unnecessary suffering, incrimination, and poisoning of joyous memory. It is sad and painful to end a relationship. No doubt about that. But we make it worse by projecting the end into the past.

So, says Solomon, labor and love without illusion. Do not expect anything to last forever. If not downsizing, then retirement. If not divorce, then death. Labor and love for the intrinsic joy of working and loving. And let the rest be.

SECURE YOURSELF A FRIEND

Here is my advice—learn from one who looked and saw.
Secure yourself a friend; two are better than one.
Do not work alone,
and learn to rejoice in another's company.

If one of you falls, the other is there to help you rise.
If it is cold, you can huddle together for warmth.
If danger threatens, two can face it better than one.
And three better still;
the cord of three strands outlasts the cord of two.

Seek out companions for work.
Seek out friends for life.
Make room for yourself and also for others.

4:9–12

We might think that a philosophy of emptiness and impermanence would lead us to a solitary, monkish existence, but this is not true of Solomon. Knowing that all things end, knowing that moments ceaselessly flow one to the other, Solomon becomes all the more appreciative of the simple joys of connecting with others.

Because life is often painful, it helps to have friends and loved ones to go to in times of need. Because life is often joyous, it helps to have friends and loved ones with whom to share the joy. Because life is impermanent, it is wise to value those relationships we have, never taking them for granted and cherishing every moment of companionship and sharing.

For some reason, the idea that life is impermanent pushes many people toward the notion that it is not worth living.

Solomon tells us just the opposite. It is because life is impermanent that each moment is so precious to us. It is because all things come to an end that each encounter is to be cherished.

A married father of four I know died recently in a freak car accident. Hundreds of people came to his funeral: family, friends, co-workers. The outpouring of emotion was almost overwhelming. Several friends of mine spoke with me just before the service and asked me what I could possibly say to the deceased's family and friends. How was I going to make this okay?

There was nothing I *could* say to make this okay. It was *not* okay. And that is how I opened the service.

"This is a horror. We are not supposed to be here doing this. There is nothing we can say to ourselves or to each other that is going to make this okay. But what we *can* do is recognize the source of our sadness and draw upon that source to find the courage to celebrate a life."

Love is the source of sorrow in this case. If this man had not been loved, his death would not have mattered. We feel pain not because a person died, but because we *loved* the person who died.

Loving people is counterintuitive. We know before we start a relationship—any relationship—that no matter how deep our love, the relationship will end. Relationships, like everything else in this world, are transient, temporary, empty of permanence. Logic would dictate that we say to ourselves, Since relationships end, and since the ending of relationships often carries with it intense pain and grief, we will choose to avoid relationships altogether.

Maybe some of us *do* say this, but most of us do not. Most of us long for relationships and are willing to endure the inevitable pain associated with them. Some very deep truths about us and life are revealed in our longing for relatedness.

First of all, the very fact that relationships happen puts the lie to the separate self. Separate selves, if they did exist, could not

145

achieve the union that is at the heart of deeply loving relationships. Separate selves cannot make room for another. They can negotiate with others, they can enter into contracts with others, but they cannot let another into themselves. Yet many of us have experienced this deep being-with and know that it is possible. And those of us who have not experienced such love can see the evidence of its possibility in the lives of those who have. We can see what such a deep connection is like and what it can do for us, how it can open us up and enliven us.

When we are deeply in love, we feel another's joy and pain. When we are deeply in love, there is no self and other, there is only self with other. I am not suggesting that we lose ourselves in others, though there are intense moments of union when in fact we do just that. I am only reminding us that we are *more* than ourselves when we are in love. This is why when a loved one dies, a piece of us dies as well. But only a piece.

There is a Jewish tradition called cutting *kriah*, which involves the wearing of a black ribbon cut almost in half as a sign of mourning. The origin of this tradition can be traced back to a time when people ripped their clothing in mourning. Over the centuries, this act became ritualized with the formal cutting of the *kriah* ribbon.

Whenever I cut *kriah* at a funeral, I remind the mourners of its significance. The ribbon represents our lives at this moment. It is cut, and the tear is left unmended. We do not go home after the funeral and sew the cloth whole again. The loss is real, the tear in our lives is real, the pain we feel is real, and we must do nothing to mask it. And yet we do not cut the ribbon in two.

The ribbon is torn but not severed. There is a part of the cloth that is untouched and whole. Love is, as Solomon tells us in his epic love poem Song of Songs, greater than death.

I ask people to honor the tear in their lives by feeling their pain and their grief. I ask them to honor the love in their lives by not imagining that death ends our connection with those we love.

If we are separate selves, each independent and alone, then when one of us dies all connection with that person is lost. But if we are part of a greater self, a larger reality that is our true nature, then when one of us dies, the connection remains. We are one before death and one after death. And we can continue to feel the presence of love and loved ones long after the body has gone.

I am not talking about some ghostly self or immortal soul, for that would imply a separate self that survives death. Neither I nor Solomon posits such a permanent self. What we are saying is that the fundamental unity of all things allows us to maintain connections even when no body is present. We are not our bodies. We are God, and God is no less whole when one of us dies.

Parents often ask me to help their children understand this way of thinking when a loved one has died. To help children with this idea, I give them a piece of string and ask them to tie a knot in it. We examine the knot carefully and come to appreciate its unique form and texture. I then ask them to tie another knot in their piece of string. We examine this second knot closely as well, discovering that it is quite different from the first. It rests on a different point on the string. It has its own shape and feel. It is bigger or smaller than the knot we first tied. Yet both knots are made of the same string, and both knots are connected by that string.

I then suggest to children that we call the first knot by their own name; the second we call by the name of the one who has recently died—Grandma, for example. Now untie Grandma's knot, I tell them. Where did that knot go? Is the string any less for the knot having been untied? Is your knot, the first knot, any less connected to the string that held Grandma's knot now that Grandma's knot is untied?

Our discussion leads to the point Solomon is making: when we look at the knots of the world—you and I and those we know and love—we know that no knot is forever. When we look at the string—the stuff of which each knot is formed—we see that the string is always there. When Grandma dies, when her knot is untied, things change, and change can hurt. But the string itself is unchanged, so the connection with Grandma is still possible. What we have to do is think in terms of the string rather than the knots, the whole rather than the parts. When we realize that we are the string, we can feel Grandma's presence even though her knot is gone. Only when we forget that all knots are just different forms of the same piece of string do we feel alone, lonely, and depressed.

The more open we are to the Whole of which we are a part, the more connected we are to the parts that the Whole manifests. Relationships help us open to the Whole. As we learn to make room for another, we learn to make room for all others. As we learn to love one, we learn to love the One.

Ecclesiastes is a book for those who wish to love. It urges us to love without fear of loss, knowing that if we love well, we will understand that there is no loss in the greater unity of God.

NO AUTHORITY

Be careful from whom you seek advice.
Do not be fooled by appearance.
Set no authority over yourself save Reality,
for in Reality alone does truth reside.

from 4:13

So many of us want a guru, someone who can tell us what is true, right, and good. We want to find the perfect master, the fully realized human being who will impart this wisdom to us. And once we are convinced that we have found our guru, we are often willing to overlook gross lapses in judgment and major moral failings in order to protect the illusion of our guru's perfect nature.

I have studied with many who are called gurus, and I have learned much from each of them. But none seemed to me to be perfect. Yet I know many students of these and other gurus who are convinced that their guru has no flaws, no limits to wisdom, and no restrictions on behavior. Indeed, some disciples I know feel that their master's moral lapses are proof of his or her having attained perfection. The very fact that the guru appears beyond the realm of human morality suggests to them that the guru is in fact a perfected being no longer bound by human morality.

Nonsense. I believe that there are enlightened masters, men and women who have dropped the last vestiges of separate self and realized the true nature of life as a manifestation of God. Such people are rare, and when they do appear in the course of history, they manifest as people of immense kindness and compassion. They can be stern and honest in their teaching and practice, but they are never exploitative in their relationships.

Kindness, not craziness, is the hallmark of a holy man or

woman. Selflessness, not selfishness, is the by-product of spiritual awakening.

I also believe that there are wise teachers who, though far from perfection, have much to teach us. Such people are far more common than the enlightened masters mentioned above, and we should be eager and grateful to learn from them. But we should not ask of such flawed teachers the perfection we expect from true gurus. Nor should we seek to cover their flaws in order to rescue a claim to enlightenment.

By all means, learn from *everyone*, but do not let claims of spiritual attainment blind us to another's ignorance, bigotry, or moral failings. In the end, it is life itself that is our guru. If we live with open eyes, we can see the truth for ourselves. This is what Solomon did, and this is what he asks us to do as well. Ecclesiastes offers us a spiritual anarchist's faith: see for yourself; experience life for yourself; taste and see that all is impermanent; experience everything under the sun and beyond, and know reality for yourself. Investigate the nature of life and living and see for yourself that all is breath upon breath, impermanent, fleeting, and yet so very precious.

DRAWING NEAR TO GOD

Be careful when drawing near to God.
Seek not to sacrifice or appease;
seek only to hear.

from 4:17

W hen we silence the self, we can listen to God. When the part is still, the Whole is known.

When I was first learning about silence and deep listening, several friends introduced me to the use of sensory-deprivation tanks. A company specializing in the use of these tanks for spiritual exploration opened up not too far from my home, and I began to float in the tanks several times each week for about forty-five minutes each time.

A sensory-deprivation tank is a fiberglass "coffin" filled with six to eight inches of specially treated salt water heated to body temperature. You undress, lie down in the tank, and close the lid. The tank is entirely light- and soundproof. The extremely high concentration of salt allows your body to float on the surface of the water, giving you the sense of weightlessness. Within moments, all external stimuli are eliminated, and you find yourself floating in what seems to be empty and limitless space.

Without external stimuli to distract you, your mind focuses on internal noise. You can, quite literally, hear your heart beating and your blood flowing. In time, these sounds also fade, and you focus on the mental chatter of the mind. All kinds of thoughts sweep through you, but because there is so little sense of *you* in the tank, these thoughts fade quickly, and you are engulfed in a great silence.

At first this quiet is hard to maintain; hallucinations are common, and sleep is hard to resist. Your dreams are so vivid that you can scarcely tell waking from sleeping. But with a bit of practice, you can float on the edge of sleep, weightless, senseless, without self and substance, and yet joyfully aware. Not aware of anything in particular, just aware. The body's limits are gone. You sense a connectedness to everything. You are everything and everything is you. You are fully present without being anyone at all. Time ends, and you float blissfully in an eternal now of empty awareness.

To some people this may sound horrible. To me it was heaven, and the results were wonderful. After every tank experience I felt lighter, more alive. The world around me seemed brighter, more vivid. Everything danced with a vitality I rarely noticed ordinarily.

I could attribute my response to the fact that I was literally coming to my senses, but there was something more to my experience than a heightened appreciation for the physical world. There was a softness to my personality that is not always present. There was a joy within and around me that is all too often lacking. I was kinder to others and more at peace with myself.

Spiritual practice manifests in this world as kindness and tranquility. This is how we measure the validity of a teacher and a teaching: Do they lead us to greater kindness toward others and deeper peace within ourselves? If they do, we should learn from them. If they do not, we should avoid them.

We do not need a sensory-deprivation tank to experience this deep silence, of course. Meditation is now my preferred practice. Each morning I sit on my meditation cushions, settle my body physically and mentally using the repetition of a simple Hebrew mantra, follow my breathing without trying to control it, and listen.

First, I listen to my body. It aches. It itches. I neither move nor scratch, and in time it aches and itches a little less. Second, I listen to my ego as it complains and spins irritating dramas about my life and the people in it. I do not respond to what I hear, and in time

152

the ego grows bored and becomes quiet. Third, I listen to my soul. It weaves wonderful visions of colors and light and symbols heavy with meaning. I do my best to wait these out, and in time they also fade away. In the end all that is left is silence. And then I listen to that.

The art of spiritual listening is the key to opening to God, as the Bible teaches us: "Give me a hearing heart," we read in 1 Kings (3:9). "Hear, O Israel, the oneness of God," we are instructed in Deuteronomy (6:4). "Listen that you may live," the prophet Isaiah (55:3) urges us. "Be still and know that I AM is God," the Psalmist sings (Psalm 46:10).

So I just listen, though by now there is no *I* that is listening. There is just listening. Just silence. Just the "still small voice of God" (1 Kings 19:12) that awakens me to my unity with God. And yours as well.

Ecclesiastes urges us to just listen. God has no need for prayer or sacrifice. God is everything and thus lacks nothing. While we may choose to pray to God because we need to articulate aloud our own struggles and desires, we should not project this need onto God.

I pray every day. I do so not to appease God, but to remind myself of life's highest truths and values. I never ask God to change what is; I only thank God for manifesting within me the power to encounter what is with grace and dignity. I never pray for something I need; I only give thanks for what I already have. I never ask God for a favor; I only give thanks for all the favors I continue to receive.

Nor do I pray with the expectation that God will answer my prayers. The prayer itself is the answer. "Dear God," I might pray, "thank you for the courage to be kind in the face of adversity." Or "Dear God, thank you for the broken heart that can cry at such pain." Or "Dear God, thank you for this love and the inner spaciousness to make room for it." Prayer is its own answer, for it reminds us of who we are, what we already have, and what we are capable of doing.

Over the years, I have written hundreds of prayers and published half a dozen prayer books, but as Solomon teaches, it is silence that is the greatest liturgy. Before composing a single verse of prayer, I sit in silence. I do not want to write from what I know but from the greater silence beyond knowing. When I tap into that, my words speak not only to me but to others, reflecting not only my truth, but the truth that each of us embodies.

When we come near to God, we should not worry about what to say. The real challenge is listening to the silence.

FREEDOM

Freedom is not bought, but seized.
Freedom is not the last step, but the first.

from 5:9–11

There is no path to freedom. There is no technique to get clear of the things that hold us fast. Freedom cannot be granted by another. It cannot be bestowed. It is proclaimed and lived, or it does not exist. Rosa Parks is my favorite model of this truth. When asked by the white bus driver to give up her seat to a white man and move to the back of the bus, she refused. She did not wait for anything to change in her life. She did not wait for anyone to tell her how to be free. She *was* free—free in that instant to move or to stay—and she chose to stay.

Many of us find this idea of freedom hard to accept. We imagine ourselves stuck, enslaved, imprisoned, victims of circumstance, heredity, culture, race, gender, or religion. Rather than affirm that we are free to do whatever needs to be done in the moment, we imagine that we must be freed from the problems and limitations of the moment before we can act at all. This belief gives us an out when it comes to acting freely: I'd like to, but I'm stuck.

Once a man came to see me who wanted to make amends to a woman he had hurt many years before. He had lost touch with her, and we talked a bit about his situation and what he would say to this woman if he could find her. After a while it was clear that he was sincere in his desire to make amends, though totally at a loss as to how to find this person. I suggested that he look her up in the phone book.

As obvious a suggestion as this was, I could see a light of recognition come into his eyes: this was a good idea, and one he had not considered previously. Do not imagine that this fellow was being disingenuous. I think he was simply blocked; he really had not thought of this. So focused was he on the deeds of the past for which he needed to make amends that he had not thought clearly about actually making amends.

Our conversation then turned to finding this woman in the phone book. He told me where she used to live and went on awhile about her old house. I stopped him after a few minutes and suggested that he take the phone book and look her up.

"Now?" he asked.

"Sure," I said, "why not now?"

"I don't know," he said. "I just thought . . . "

"You just thought we could *talk* about calling her instead of calling her and that somehow this talking about it would be the same as doing it. Sorry, it doesn't work that way." I tossed him the white pages and waited as he looked to see if she was listed.

She was indeed—and still living at the same address. He wanted to talk about that for a while, but I was not buying. Instead, I got up from my desk and said, "Sit in my chair and call her now." He did.

Thinking that freedom means "freedom from" rather than "freedom to" is the trap into which many of us fall. We imagine that we cannot do anything until we are happy and problem-free.

A dentist I know has written a delightful little book with an unfortunate title: *Life Without Stress*. There *is* no life without stress. Stress is essential to life. Yes, too much stress can kill us, but no stress at all is just as deadly. Indeed, the only time we are completely without stress is when we are dead.

Stress and problems are part of life. Trying to eliminate all stress and all problems is a waste of energy—energy that we need to deal constructively with stress and problems.

This is the trap that Ecclesiastes warns us against. If we wait until we are stress- and problem-free before we enjoy life, we will wait forever. The freedom that Solomon speaks of is the freedom that comes from knowing the transience of both joy and suffering, blessings and problems. With this knowledge, he tells us, we are free to be joyous and miserable as the moment requires, without clinging to the former or bemoaning the latter. We are free simply to be present to each moment as it comes, and to engage it with integrity.

THE MORE YOU HAVE

The more you have, the more you are hounded.
The more you have, the more you have to defend;
and you will have no time for appreciation and joy.

from 5:9–11

When Solomon warns us of the snare of possessions, do not think he is speaking only of things. Ideas, ideals, and theories can snare us no less than property.

A young man I know sees himself as a spiritual seeker, modeling himself after a romanticized vision of what he thinks the Buddha must have been like. He owns very little and talks softly. Indeed, he can pack everything he owns into a single duffel bag and take to the road anytime he pleases. I know this, because he never tires of telling me.

This young man is as trapped in the idea of *not* owning as many of us are trapped in the idea of owning. There is nothing wrong with owning things (or not owning them). What is wrong is when things (or the lack of things) own us.

Ecclesiastes is not taking a stand against material things. Remember, Solomon celebrated the joy he received from material goods. Ecclesiastes is simply reminding us that ownership carries a price. One very sound guideline I derive from Ecclesiastes regarding ownership is this: if something I own adds beauty and peace to my life, I keep it; if not, I give it away. Before I buy something, I ask if it will add beauty and peace to my life.

"The more you have, the more you have to defend." This is true not only of things. It is true of feelings, opinions, and ideas as well. The more invested we are in what we have, the more defensive we feel a need to be. And being defensive makes us nervous, anxious, and fearful.

When I was a young man, I used to think I had to have an opinion on everything. I actually made a list of all the issues about which I should have an opinion. I worked up formal statements on the issues of the day and waited anxiously for opportunities to share them.

Sometimes my opinions made sense; most often, however, they reflected muddled thinking and my adolescent lack of understanding. And yet when someone disagreed with me, I felt honor-bound to defend my opinion. Even when I knew that the other person was wiser in some particular matter than I was, I still clung passionately to my original idea. It was a matter of pride, of self-esteem, of self-defense.

Later, when I had had time to reflect on my opponent's comments, I would adjust my thinking and sharpen my opinion; but the next time I offered it, I would defend this revised opinion with the same intensity with which I had defended the previous opinion.

It has taken me quite some time to be comfortable with the words "I don't know," yet now I find them among the most liberating sentences I utter. Admitting that I do not know something, and recognizing that much of what I claim to know is simply oft-repeated opinion, frees me from the need to defend my ideas or myself.

I write and lecture extensively, and I take a lot of pleasure in exploring new ideas and making bold statements. But I no longer feel the need to defend any of these. If I am right in what I say, fine. If my thinking proves to be flawed, that too is fine—and most of the time I am open to learning where I went wrong. This attitude allows me to think more freely and creatively, knowing that everything I say is a work in progress.

Solomon tells us to live without too much stuff or too many fixed ideas. What we should do, he says, is retract the energy we expend on protecting our things and our ideas from their inevitable demise. We should instead enjoy what we have while we have it, and then move on.

EMPTY WE ENTER

Empty we enter; empty we depart.
You waste your time trying to find fullness in things or desires.
What fullness there is arises of its own accord
when you learn to live simply with whatever each moment
    brings.

from 5:12–15

Fulfillment comes from being present to the moment. That is all we have. If we are distracted from the moment, we miss the only place in which we can find fulfillment. This is so clear that we might think it would be axiomatic. Yet it is not. Sometimes it takes an extreme situation to reveal this simple truth. Death is often that situation.

Not long ago I received an emergency call from a woman whose father was in the last stages of dying. She wanted a rabbi present, had heard of me, and begged me to rush to the hospital to see her dad.

When I got there, I found the daughter standing over her father's bed and talking quietly with him. I stepped into the room, keeping toward the back. He was telling her how much he loved her, and how proud he was of her and what she had done with her life. Then he told her it was time for him to go. He closed his eyes and died.

She turned to me and smiled, thanked me for coming, and then sat down in a chair next to her father's hospital bed. After a few minutes of silence, I asked her if she wanted to call a nurse to attend to her father. "No," she said, "he'll be back in a minute or two."

I masked my shock at her words with a tentative smile. She just was not ready to let his death be real to her, I thought. But what did I know? Within five minutes her father *was* back. He coughed a bit, opened his eyes, and said, "What am I still doing here?"

His daughter smiled as she took his hand, and they talked some more.

We stepped out of the room a little later and she explained to me that he had done this a dozen times in the last two days. He would call her to him, tell her how much he loved and cherished her, and then close his eyes to die. But then he would not die. He kept coming back.

She laughed as she told me this. She was so happy that he wanted to make sure she knew with his dying breath how much he loved her. He did not want any doubts or unfinished business. I told her that her dad was fulfilling the rabbinic obligation to make peace with life one day before we die. "Yes," she said, "he was doing that."

Just then he called her in again. I accompanied her and listened as he again told her how he felt. He turned his head slightly in my direction and said that he was not afraid to die because he was not ashamed of how he had lived. He then asked me to say a prayer. I recited the *Viddui*, a prayer offering forgiveness to and requesting forgiveness from everyone he had touched in his life. He thanked me for the prayer and for coming to see him. He turned back to his daughter, smiled, closed his eyes, and died.

This time he did not come back. There was no need. He had made peace with his life, leaving nothing undone and nothing unsaid.

FORTRESS AGAINST LOSS

Do not build a fortress against loss
or lay siege to eternity.
Rather, open your eyes to the wonder of the fleeting
and make of each moment an opportunity to do what needs
    doing.

from 5:17–19

I cannot count the number of deaths I have attended. Each is unique; no two people die alike, and no two people survive alike. And the interplay of the dying and the surviving never matches the neat scenarios I studied in seminary. There is only death and survival, both of which can be characterized by luminosity.

Much of the dying I have witnessed has been with terminally ill people, most of whom are unconscious of their dying. The medications they are given allow them to seemingly sleep right through one of the most transformative moments of their existence. Yet even in these sleeping transformations there is an instant of light and lightness where the body sighs into death and the temporary separate self surrenders to the One who is all. Despite the suffering of the survivors, they too can feel the love that is so often present at the moment of death.

On one level there may be the relief that the suffering is over— both the suffering of the deceased and the suffering of those waiting for the inevitable. On another level there may be a sense of joy, even in the midst of grief. Often this is accompanied by soft laughter mixed with tears. People are embarrassed when this happens—after all, death is not a time for laughter. Yet the laughter is there. Why? Because at some deep though hidden level, we know that death is a returning home, and homecoming can be a sweet and joyous thing.

The very first death I attended was that of a young man suffering from a disease that had left him horribly twisted and in constant pain. The boy's family and I were called by one of the boy's physicians and told that his death was imminent. We gathered at the hospital and sat quietly waiting for the boy to die. He slept, his breathing loud and raspy. Sometimes he stopped breathing completely, and we would jump up from our chairs to see if he had died. Then his chest would heave and he would breathe once more.

It was during one of these breathless pauses that something totally unexpected happened. The boy stopped breathing for a moment and then jolted upright in bed. Resuming breathing, he opened his eyes and smiled at everyone in the room. His voice dry and hoarse, he forced himself to speak: "I found it," he said. And then he died.

Whatever he found had brought him peace. And his sharing of that peace brought us a bit of peace as well.

A HOUSE OF MOURNING;
A HOUSE OF FEASTING

Better to go to a house of mourning
than to a house of feasting.
In the first there is the silence of death,
the transience of life, the tears of loss and letting go.
This is the world, its simplicity and its suffering.
In the other there is only blind hunger,
forced laughter, false joy—
a desperate filling up of that which is forever emptying.

from 7:1–2

If we are attuned to it, we can often sense an energy in a house of mourning that hovers at the edge of joy—the deep joy and equanimity that come when we accept the fleetingness of life and thereby open ourselves to its wonders. As we walk among the mourners, we are reminded of what really matters: family, friends, caring, love. Death puts life in perspective and reminds us not to waste the precious time we have on bitterness.

It is customary for Jewish mourners to open their homes to visitors after a funeral. I have attended hundreds of these gatherings over the twenty-plus years of my work as a rabbi. While not every house of mourning can be or needs to be a house of reconciliation, I rarely fail to sense a renewed and deepened sense of compassion among the mourners.

On one such occasion I witnessed a profound transformation in a couple whose divorce, while long final, had created a hatred that continued to consume them both. They had not spoken to each other in four years, though their respective lawyers maintained a vicarious conversation on their behalf. They were together at the funeral of a mutual friend and found themselves face to face during a condolence visit to the deceased's wife.

I watched as they glared at each other. I imagined that I could see their brains churning to find just the right word to cause the other pain. Before either could speak, however, the four-year-old son of the deceased ran between them. For some reason he stopped, took hold of their legs as if they were pillars, and looked up into their faces. Totally focused, he looked intently at first one and then the other. All of a sudden he screamed out, "Hug!" I expected him to lift up his arms to be picked up, but instead he let go of their legs and ran off.

Was he asking for a hug or demanding that they hug? Who knows. But the couple was startled—I would say startled to the point of forgetting to rehearse their hatred. For a moment their faces softened and they forgot their plan to verbally injure each other. They looked at each other without dragging the hatred of the past into the freshness of the moment. They smiled, said a few gentle words to each other, and moved on to talk with other visitors.

Yes, it would have been a better story if they had suddenly fallen into each other's arms, asking for forgiveness and resolving years of bitter dispute. But then it would have been a *story* and not what really happened. What really happened, however, was enough. Within three months their lawyers had settled what everyone had expected would evolve into an endless legal battle; and while they are in no way friends today, they no longer hate each other or seek to do each other harm.

They saw something in that house of mourning—not something in the child, but something in themselves. They saw their own mortality, their own impermanence, their own preciousness, and they knew that they were wasting their life energies by perpetuating their hatred.

I suspect that a similar encounter would have been less

possible at a wedding, which is one reason that Solomon prefers mourning to feasting.

Weddings and funerals have a very different energy. Besides the obvious lightness at the one and seriousness at the other, there is a more subtle difference—one that Solomon suggests makes the latter preferable to the former.

At a wedding the energy is often rushed and forced. There is a superficiality to the festivities and, if we look closely enough, a tinge of fear as well. Will Uncle Fred embarrass us again? Will Aunt Martha lose her dignity to the champagne? Will Carla and Murray start a scene? Will the marriage last?

At a wedding there is a desire to control. We want the event to be perfect, and we expect nothing less than perfection from the people we have hired to make it perfect. We rehearse, we choreograph, we stage, we pose—we have an image in our minds of what the perfect wedding is supposed to be, and we do our best to see that we get it.

At a funeral the energy is anything but rushed, and we let go of perfection. There is no image of the perfect funeral that we are seeking to impose on our reality. There are only death, grief, and the rolling emotions that threaten to knock us off our feet. We lack both the energy and the desire to control. It just does not matter.

Free from the desire to control, we are free to feel whatever it is we feel. Free from the need to imitate someone else's way of grieving, we are free to grieve in our own way. Family dynamics follow us wherever we go, of course, but at a funeral the introspective nature of death pulls us toward a deeper level of consideration. This is why Solomon values mourning over feasting.

When feasting, we too often stuff ourselves to cover the inner fear that haunts us. When mourning, we draw on that fear and give it voice. Drawing on that fear honors it, and in honoring it we begin to make peace with it.

DO NOT COMPARE

Do not compare one day to another.
Make what you can of each day as it is.

from 7:10–12

I used to expect a certain continuity from one day to the next.
The person I was yesterday should be the person I am today.
The flavor of yesterday's events should carry over into today. If I
was sad yesterday, I should be sad today. If I was happy yesterday,
I should be happy today.

I know this is silly. Life would be intolerable if yesterday
defined today. Life is bearable only because today has the potential
to be unlike yesterday.

When we compare one day to the next, we are looking for
continuity. But continuity is not intrinsic to the moment; it is an
arbitrary construct we impose on the moment. So stop
comparing, says Solomon. Stop looking for and imposing
continuity. Accept the radical discontinuity of life: we are new
each moment, free to be different—if different is what is required.

This idea is powerfully liberating. We are not enslaved to the
past. We are created fresh each moment. If I was angry with
someone yesterday, I need not be so today. Rather than let the
past determine what is appropriate in the present, says Solomon,
we ought to attend to the present, ascertaining from it the right
way to be, here and now. Our challenge is to be not contiguous
with the past but congruent with the present.

ACCEPTANCE

Knowledge guards the mind from deception.
Wealth protects the body from hunger.
But only acceptance of impermanence brings tranquility.

from 7:10–12

There is value in being knowledgeable, in having lots of facts at one's fingertips. Knowledge, which allows us to distinguish truth from falsehood, fact from fiction, guards us from deceptive ideas and images. Being knowledgeable, however, is not the same as being wise. Wisdom comes not from knowing the *facts* of life but from knowing the *way* of life: its nature as a temporary manifestation of the one reality, God.

Some of the wisest teachers I have known have lacked formal education. Though short on book-learning, they have seen into the hearts of people; they have been able to point people in the direction of inner transformation and healing; they have had the ability to expound on the interconnection of all things in a profound yet simple manner.

Does that mean that accumulating knowledge is wrong or useless? No. It means only that knowledge is not to be confused with wisdom.

Just as there is nothing wrong with knowledge, there is nothing wrong with wealth. I have friends who judge people's moral worth by how much or little they have. According to this standard of morality, the wealthier you are, the meaner and more immoral you must be; the poorer you are, the more righteous you must be. This is nonsense. I suspect that such a perspective is rooted more in jealously than in anything else.

I have other friends who believe that wealth is a sign of blessing by God. The more you have, the more God loves you. This idea is no less irrational than the other. How much or how little money we have tells nothing about our character. What matters is how we earn our money and how we spend it. Wealth itself is neutral.

Neither knowledge nor wealth can protect us from the reality of life's intrinsic impermanence. That does not mean there is no value to them, however. When we learn because we want to know something, and earn because we want to purchase something, we are using knowledge and wealth as they are meant to be used. Problems arise only when we imagine that either of these activities can help us escape the transience of our own existence. The impermanence of life is a problem only if we insist that life should be permanent. Accept life for what it is, and we can learn and earn with tranquility and peace.

WHEN YOU DO RIGHT,
WHEN YOU DO WRONG

When you do right, rejoice,
but do not proclaim yourself righteous.
This was but one moment;
in the next you may do differently.

When you do wrong, reflect,
but do not call yourself evil.
This was but one moment;
in the next you can do differently.

from 7:13–14

I know lots of people—professional clergy, mostly—who love to
debate whether humans are essentially good or essentially evil.
I find the choice unacceptable. People are capable of both good
and evil. Why assume that one is more *essential* than the other? If
good people can do evil and evil people can do good, I have to keep
on my toes with people regardless of my thoughts on their
essential nature. After all, I would rather run into a bad person on
a good day than a good person on a bad day.

Making assumptions about human nature is not only beside
the point, it can be dangerous. You must know at least one nasty
person who is convinced that people are basically good (and is
eager to offer him- or herself as a prime exemplar). I know half a
dozen people who are convinced that they are righteous and that,
by definition, whatever they do is righteous. These are the sort of
people who preface hurtful statements with "I have to be honest."
Why do they have to be honest? Maybe silence is the wiser choice.

When you do good, feel good. When you do bad, feel bad. But
do not make the mistake of identifying with either good or bad.

NO REWARD, NO PUNISHMENT

There is no reward. There is no punishment.
There is only the coming and going of life.

from 7:15–16

This is a difficult idea for many of us to accept. After all, from childhood on we have been taught to think in terms of reward and punishment. Our parents certainly operated on the reward-punishment plan, and our clergy insisted that God did the same. Be good, do good, and Mom and God will see that we get what we want. Yet good things happen to bad people. And bad things happen to good people. If we were to run a tally, in the end we might find that good and bad happen more or less equally to most people, regardless of what they do and how they live. So why bother being good?

When I talk with children about being good, I often ask them to stand up and stomp their right foot on their left foot with all their might. Hardly anyone does this; and those few that do, do so gingerly and for laughs. I then ask the children why they hesitate to do as I asked.

"Because it's stupid," someone inevitably says. "I'd be hurting myself."

Exactly. Now the challenge is to expand our sense of self to include everyone else. If we would not stomp on our own foot, why stomp on someone else's foot? Yet as long as we believe that there *is* someone else—someone separate from us, that is—we will find a way to rationalize stomping. When we realize that the world is empty of separate selves, that we are all part of the One Self, God, then we would no more hurt another person than we would hurt ourselves.

The more real unity becomes to us, the more connected we

feel with others. The more connected we feel with others, the more compassionately we act toward them. When people become real to us as living human beings, as manifestations of God, we cannot exploit or harm them. We have to strip people of their humanness and their divinity before we can do harm to them. That is why every conflict, whether it is between neighbors or nations, is accompanied by a propaganda campaign designed to turn people into enemies by insisting that they are alien, separate, and other.

Yet nothing is alien, separate, and other. We are one. To hurt another is to hurt ourselves. To wage war against "them" is to make war against "us." Thus we do harm to the extent that we buy the lie of separateness. See through the illusion, and peace will prevail.

DESTINY

There is no power over destiny;
neither the wicked nor the wise control it.

from 8:9–13

There are two bumper stickers I often see pasted on the backs of cars. One reads *Miracles Happen*. The other says *Shit Happens*. I agree with both, though I believe that each tells only half the story. I would like to create a bumper sticker that reads *Shit Happens—What A Miracle!*

Miracles Happen reminds us of all the good that we encounter. *Shit Happens* reminds us of all the crap that we encounter. Life is not a matter of noticing the one and avoiding the other. It is a matter of accepting both. The miracle is not that good stuff happens. The miracle is that anything happens at all.

Jewish spiritual practice includes the recitation of one hundred blessings every day—affirmations of thanksgiving for what happens to us during the day. Some of these are common, such as blessings over food. Some are more rare, such as blessings when seeing a rainbow, a scholar, or an old friend after a long absence. There are even blessings for the horrible things that happen to us. The practice of saying blessings reminds us that whatever happens to us is a gift—even the things we wish we could return.

ILLUSION

Just as a fish is taken in a net,
just as a bird is caught in a snare,
so are you trapped in the illusion of permanence.

from 9:11–12

One trap into which we all too easily fall is the trap of permanence. We have heard Solomon repeat this over and over again. Why? Because he knows that most of us will not get it the first time around. Uncomfortable with the truth of our own transience, we need to have it pointed out to us over and over again.

One of the tools I use to help bring this point to life for people in my workshops and retreats is a bucket with tiny holes drilled in the bottom. When the workshops are held in places where there is a pool, I bring my buckets with me and take the students out to the pool.

The students break up into small teams. I give each team a bucket and an eight-ounce plastic cup and station each team a few feet from the pool. The bucket, I explain, represents the self. The more full the bucket becomes, the more permanence the self has. What I ask each team to do is place the bucket on the ground, run to the pool, fill the cup with water, run back to the bucket, and pour the water into the bucket in order to fill the bucket as high as they can.

I set a timer and ring a bell to get the game going. Each team sends a runner to the pool to fill the cup, race back, and pour the contents into the bucket. Water trickles out the bottom of the bucket, but slowly enough that a runner who moves fast can actually get ahead of the leak and fill the bucket fairly full. But if she stops, the bucket empties out. As each runner tires, a new team member takes over.

When the timer buzzes and the exercise ends, all the running and pouring cease and I check each bucket to see which team has won. I do so at a leisurely pace so that by the time I look at the first bucket all of the buckets are empty. We are *all* losers. The game is rigged; we cannot win. There is no permanence.

Then I ask for alternative ways to fill the bucket. After a few minutes someone usually gets the bright idea of tossing the bucket in the pool. With that method, the bucket fills with water with no effort at all.

Our desire for permanence requires a never-ending effort that drives us to exhaustion. If we stop to catch our breath, the bucket empties; we die. So we never stop, never catch our breath—and yet we die just the same. We are trapped in the idea of having a permanent and separate self. And the idea is killing us.

The alternative is to give up the illusion of separateness and permanence and immerse ourselves in the pool, in the Whole of which we are each a part. When we do this, we discover that while each self is temporary, the Source of all selves is not. This awakening does not change the fact of our impermanence, but it does remove the need to defend against it. And removing the need to defend ourselves against reality allows us to use our energies to more effectively attend to reality.

An elderly man who took one of my workshops put it this way in a thank-you note he emailed to me shortly after returning home from the workshop:

My whole life has been an effort to prove my self-worth. Everything I have done and everything I own seems to me to be an attempt to say to the world: I exist, I matter, I will be remembered. After this weekend, however, I feel differently. I don't begrudge the past, but I am no longer driven by the same urge. I don't have to prove my self-worth; I only have to act in a worthwhile manner. I don't have to prove I matter; I only have to do things that matter. I don't have to be remembered; I just have to remember what I really am—a bit of God living here and now in service to all.

CHOOSE A PATH TO FOLLOW

Even if the foolish choose a path to follow,
it is quickly abandoned as another suddenly appears more
alluring.

from 10:1–3

There are a lot of people who shuttle from seminar to workshop to retreat, always collecting spiritual experiences. And those of us who teach on the spirituality circuit are happy to sell these experiences to them. Yet true spirituality is not about experiences, no matter how sublime. True spirituality is about seeing through the illusion of separateness and permanence and living the compassion that fills us when we *do* see through it.

Those of us who dare to teach in this field must be very clear, both with ourselves and with our students: there is no path to God because there is no separation from God. All we need to do is attend to the truth in each moment, and we will naturally awaken to the fact that each of us is a part of (rather than apart from) God.

If we are honest about this, we will never make ourselves or our words the point of our work. We are lenses through which other people may see the true nature of things as extensions of God. If we cloud the lens with our own egos, we will direct students' attention away from God and to ourselves. We will allow students to make us—rather than the moment—the center of attention. We will use seekers to feed our egos. We will make of ourselves and our teachings altars upon which to sacrifice the truth.

Students and teachers must work together to keep each other in the moment. Students must expect nothing from their teachers except a compassionate and honest pointing to the moment. Teachers must expect nothing from their students except a compassionate and honest attending to the moment. It is the moment, not the student or the teacher, that harbors the truth.

LIVE IN AWE

Life itself is wonder.
As long as you live,
live in awe.
And remember—
some days are bright, others are dark,
and both are life's shadow play.
Make no snare for the light;
there is no salvation in holding on.
Make no drama of the dark;
there is no reward for suffering.
Rather, embrace each as it is,
knowing that true joy
resides in serving each moment in peace.

from 11:7–8

How many of us expect a reward for suffering? I catch myself in this trap all the time. I put myself out for someone and then expect a payback—maybe a simple thank-you or a favor in return. And when that payback is not forthcoming, I am hurt and often angry. I feel ripped off.

This is needless suffering. We must do what we do because it has to be done. We must take comfort in the doing and leave the rest alone. Otherwise, we find ourselves trapped in our own self-importance. And where does self-importance come from? From the sense that we have an important self in the first place. Traps within traps within traps.

There is a Hasidic teaching that says that for every lock there is a key, but God loves the thief who breaks the lock. In other words, we could spend a lifetime working on each trap one at a time, seeking the key that would open each lock and free us to work on the next one. Or we could realize that the whole mess is predicated on a single lock that we must break without a key.

That lock, that trap, is the idea that we exist as separate selves. And the breaking of that lock comes not from amassing more and more ideas about self; rather, it comes from meditating to the point where the self breaks, the lock shatters, and the trap springs open of its own accord.

It all comes down to practice. Talk is fine. Ideas are interesting. But practice is what counts. There are lots of meditation practices, and I urge you to find one and stick with it. I have written at length about mine in a book called *Minyan*. The essence of my practice, the heart of what I teach, comes from the prophet Micah, who said, "What does God require? Just this: Do justly, act kindly, and walk humbly with your God" (Micah 6:8).

And this is what I suggest we strive to do. In doing justly, we seek to live honestly and carefully, doing no harm, saying what we mean, and doing what we say. In acting kindly, we put others first much of the time. In walking humbly, we make room for God in our lives by emptying the self of itself. How?

I know only one way: meditation. Sitting comfortably, breathing easily, repeating a sacred phrase over and over again to quiet the mind, and listening. Listening to the self as it chatters itself into existence. When we just listen without getting caught up in the chatter, just watch without getting lost in the drama, we begin to discern a greater sense of who we are. In time—and it takes *lots* of time—we discover that this greater self is God, the Whole of which we are a part. As the sages of all the world's religions tell us, after many years we might, even if only for a moment, slip so completely into that One that we are gone.

When we return, we will never be the same again.

A WHOLE AND HOLY WORLD

So when all is said, remember this:
open your mind to wonder,
your heart to compassion,
and your hand to justice,
that you fashion a whole and holy world.

from 12:9–14

Here is the summation of Solomon's teaching. Each moment is a precious expression of God. Never repeating, it comes only to pass away. If we are to live well, we must do so here and now, for that is all there is. Pay attention to this moment, and this moment again. Do not control it, judge it, cling to it, or flee from it. Just be with it, in it, as it. Attending to the moment, we see the wonder that surrounds and fills us.

Accepting impermanence, we honor and respect our bodies, our minds, our hearts, our relationships, and everything that comes our way. Engaging each moment without fear or hesitation, we open ourselves to the full range of feeling, knowing that we are always free to act wisely.

Recognizing the interdependence of all things, we act justly, gracefully, and compassionately in every situation. Knowing that all is God, we cling to nothing and rejoice in everything. We take pleasure in the moment as we might enjoy a game—a precious, sacred game—knowing that if we play with open hearts and open minds, we can bring a bit of joy and comfort to all we meet and in this way make the world a little more loving for our having been born into it.